An Alarming Accident

OR EVERY GLASS TELLS A STORY

The forgotten engraved glass of North East England

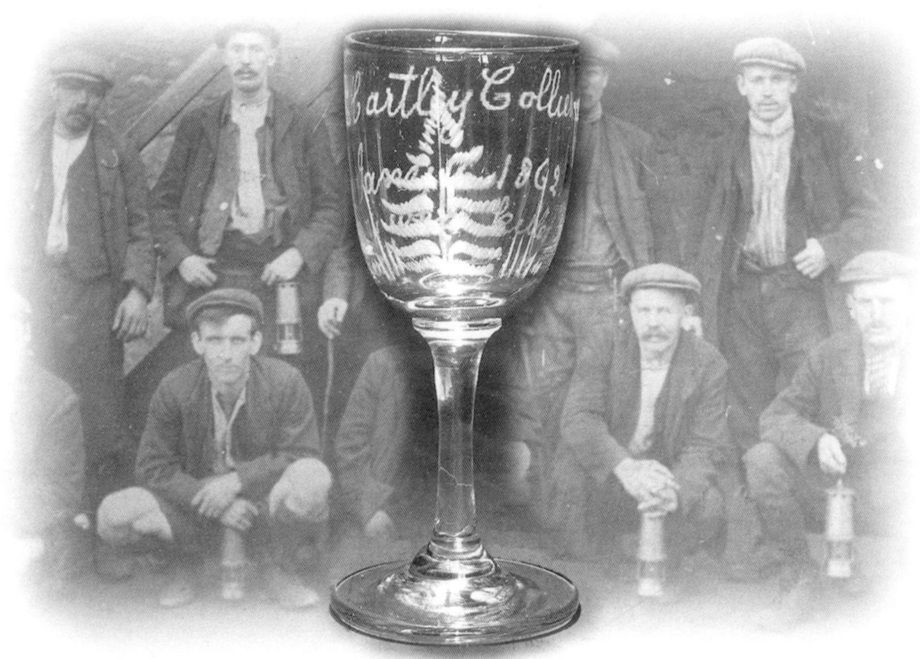

John Brooks and William Cowan

Tyne Bridge Publishing

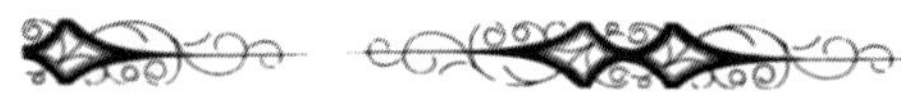

Authors' acknowledgements

It is a pleasure to acknowledge the assistance that we have received from so many sources. Among them are the staff of Alnwick, Blyth, Durham City, Morpeth, Newcastle upon Tyne, North Tyneside, South Tyneside, Stanley and Sunderland Libraries.

Museum staff who have offered their advice and support include Rosemary Allan (Beamish Museum), Shauna Gregg (Sunderland Museum), Roger Dodsworth (Broadfield House Glass Museum) and especially Deborah Moffat (Woodhorn Museum).

Our thanks are due to Jackie Reffin and Paul Kettle, private collectors who have allowed us to photograph and record glasses in their collections.

Assistance and support in other areas of expertise has come from Bob Balmer and Gordon Smith (erudite local historians), Anna Flowers, Kevin White, Pamela and Shelagh.

Tyne Bridge Publishing would like to thank Christie's Images, Tyne & Wear Archives, and Tyne & Wear Museums for their kind assistance.

The photographs of the glasses are by John Brooks unless otherwise indicated. Archive photographs are from the collections of Newcastle Libraries unless otherwise indicated.

Published by
City of Newcastle upon Tyne
Newcastle Libraries & Information Service
Tyne Bridge Publishing
2008

www.tynebridgepublishing.co.uk

ISBN: 978 1857951240

Printed by Printers (Coast) Ltd, Newcastle upon Tyne

CONTENTS

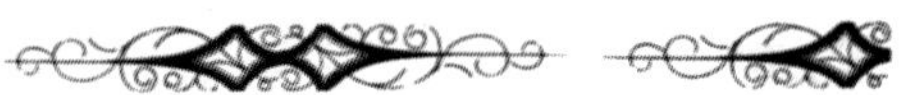

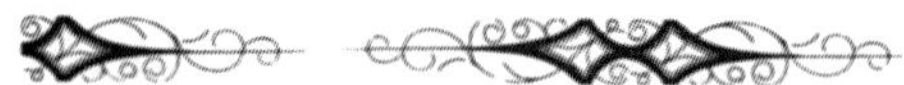

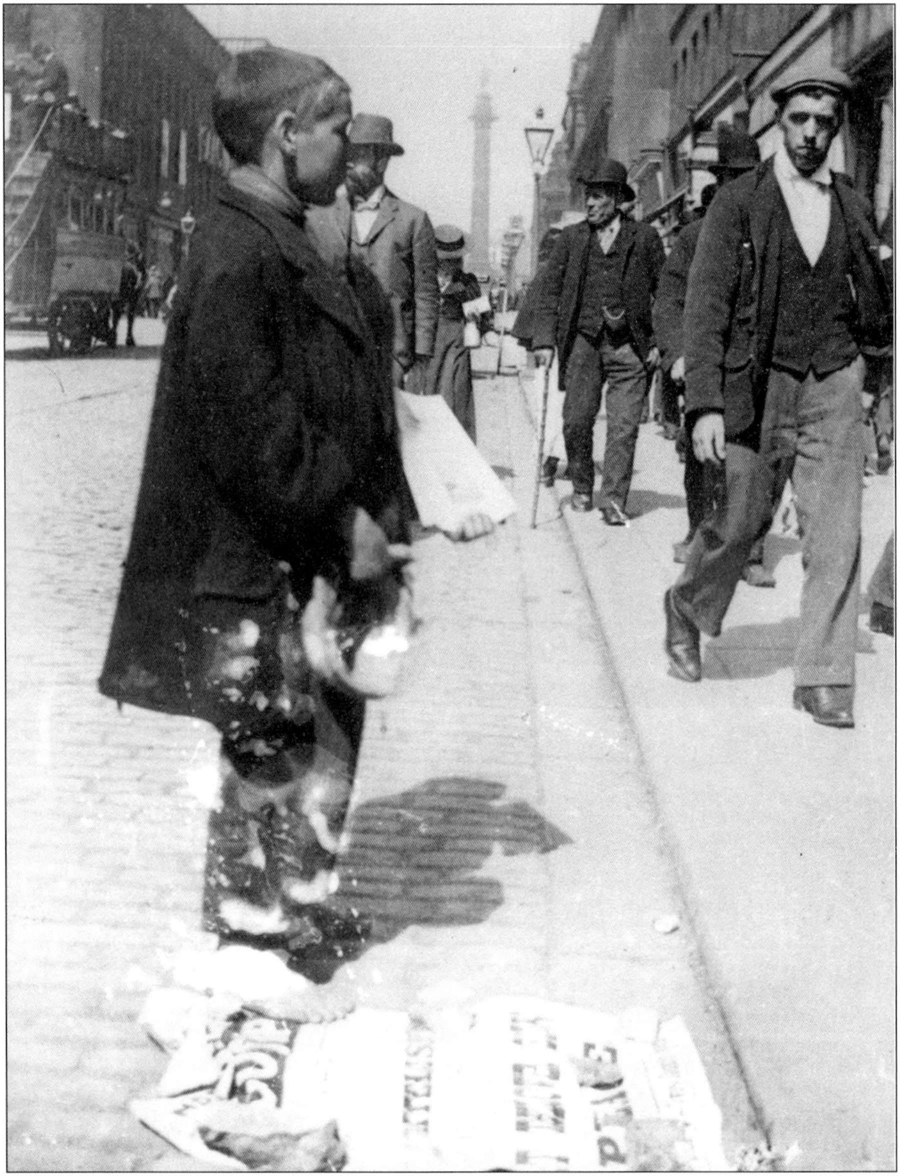

Selling the news: Grainger Street, Newcastle, 1898.

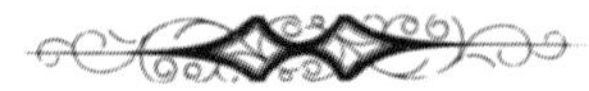
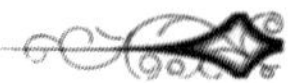

STORIES FROM THE PAST

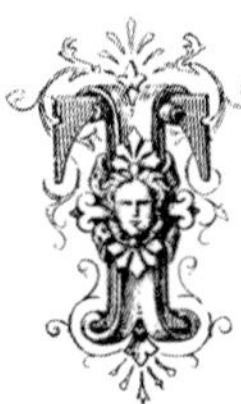

he popular image of the engraved glass of the North East of England is perhaps best exemplified by the rummers that commemorate the Sunderland Bridge. They are usually engraved with a view of a sailing ship passing beneath the cast iron bridge over the River Wear and one is immediately struck by the generally high quality of the engraving. They date from about 1800-1850 and were produced as souvenirs of a visit to what was universally considered to be a remarkable feat of engineering. Glasses bearing views of the bridges over the River Tyne and other subjects, engraved to an equally high standard, may be seen in the Laing Art Gallery in Newcastle and at Sunderland Museum.

There is, however, another larger group of glasses which also originated in the North East that we think has been largely overlooked because the engraving is generally of indifferent quality and the glasses themselves are unremarkable. They appear to be peculiar to the North East in that they commemorate a wide variety of events concerning the life and times of the inhabitants of the area.

A number of these glasses record mining accidents and passing reference has been made to them by previous writers who usually refer to them as 'Disaster Glasses' but they also record events and topics embracing the whole spectrum of life in the area during the period from about 1880 up to the first world war.

This book is the result of more than 20 years of research by the authors into the events recorded on these glasses. John Brooks, who has no connection with the North East, first became fascinated by them when he came across

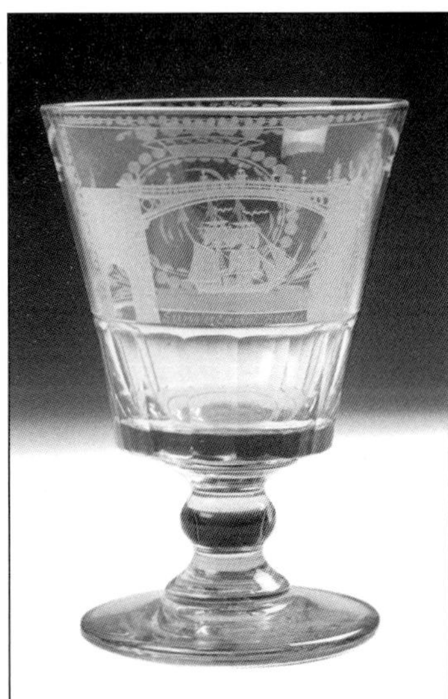

A finely engraved rummer made by White, Young & Tuer (Wear Glassworks) Sunderland, 1820-1850.

Sunderland Museum & Winter Gardens, Tyne & Wear Museums

A more modest glass celebrates Seaton Sluice bridge, 1894.

examples in the course of his business as a dealer in antique glass. Bill Cowan is a collector who long ago realised how much these little glasses have to tell us. Because he has the advantage of living in the area he has been responsible for most of the research in the public records.

What started out of curiosity led us to a re-discovery of the hard life endured by most working class people in the late 19th century, particularly the mining community of the North East, and we hope that by resurrecting many of these events readers will be reminded of, and pay due respect to, their hardy and indomitable forbears.

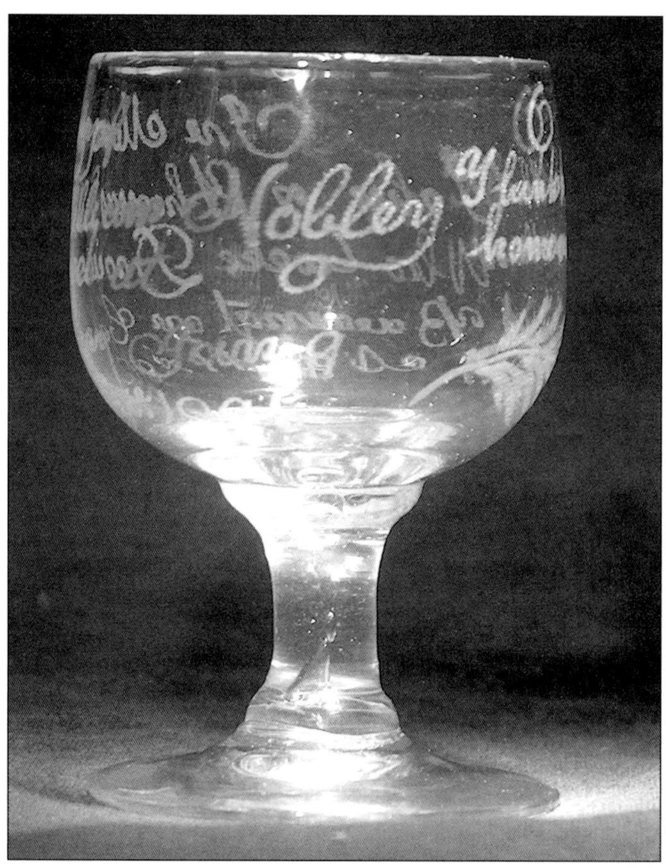

A pub glass commemorating the deaths of John and Thomas William Nobley who drowned in 1895.

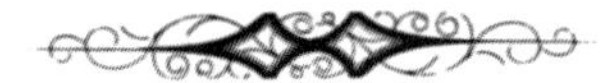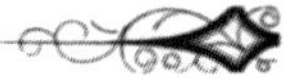

DISASTER GLASSES

he origins of this book lie in the discovery of a small, nondescript pub glass engraved with the inscription, *In Memory of John & Thomas William Nobley Who Were Drowned at Barrington Colliery Jan 9 1895 Age 11 & 8 Years*. At that point one could only speculate on whether they had been working in the colliery or playing around a disused mine shaft and fallen into it. A couple of years later a similar glass turned up with the inscription *Hetton Colliery Explosion 20.12.1860 22 Lives Lost*. The similarity of the style of engraving and the reference to mining led to speculation about whether there was any connection with the earlier find. Since the second one commemorated what was obviously a serious accident that must have been publicly recorded, it did not take too much effort to discover that both Hetton and Barrington Collieries were in the North East of England.

Research into subsequent finds of glasses inscribed with references to other accidents revealed that they all referred to mines in the Durham and Northumberland coalfields. It became obvious that it must have been common practice in North East England to commemorate mining accidents on glass and, because many of the inscriptions include the word 'Disaster', they have generally become known amongst collectors as 'Disaster Glasses'. It became apparent that similar glasses, bearing a variety of other inscriptions unconnected with mining, must have originated in the same area.

The catalogue of inscriptions steadily grew and it soon became clear that they also covered non-accidental events relating to mining as well as a great variety of other events entirely unrelated to mining. Some of them recorded tragedies, such as the Victoria Hall disaster in Sunderland. Other glasses related to loss of life at sea or the deaths of individuals, both well-known locally and unknown. Yet another group recorded public events of local or national importance. What little has been published about these glasses has tended to refer only to the mining accidents, no doubt because of their dramatic nature and the fact that they can all be readily linked by a common theme. What seems to have escaped notice is the larger body of other inscribed glasses which can be associated with so many other aspects of life in the North East. In the course of this book we shall explore some of the human stories behind many of the inscriptions.

The reader may wonder what is special about these glasses given that they are mostly of poor quality with indifferent engraving, since many other glasses produced in other parts of the British Isles also recorded people and events. That is true, of course, but what we believe distinguishes these glasses from all others is their consistency of style and decoration and the wide range of local events they commemorate that enables them to be uniquely identified with the North East of England. They open a window for us on to the lives of a largely working class society that might otherwise not be remembered.

We have discovered no consistent evidence of glasses that commemorate mining accidents elsewhere in England, other than those for Whitehaven (37) and Bolton (38). Both these major disasters, occurring in 1910, made national headlines so it is not surprising that they should evoke some response from the North Eastern engravers at a time when other national events were being widely commemorated in the North East. Even in other major industrial and glass making areas of the country like Birmingham and Lancashire there appears to have been no consistent pattern of using glass in this way.

It is interesting to speculate on the reasons why this custom should have developed exclusively in the North East; this will be considered in a later chapter but it may well be connected with the close-knit nature of mining communities, the hardship of their daily lives and their reliance on each other.

In the text we have tried to preserve the style of the inscriptions with italics to represent cursive script and, wherever our records permit, with '/' denoting a line break to indicate the layout of the inscription on the glass. We have also preserved the use of upper and lower case characters although some inscriptions may not have been properly transcribed in our earliest records before the significance of the whole group became apparent. A number in brackets following a reference to a glass or an inscription refers to its unique entry in Tables 1-5 at the end of the book. In addition to the text recording the event, the majority of glasses also feature stylised foliage such as a fern or a clover leaf engraved on the reverse. Some glasses recording deaths or disasters also include other comments such as *Rock of Ages* on the reverse while others, recording drowning, depict a boat on the reverse. These extra inscriptions and features will be discussed in a later chapter when we consider the engravers themselves.

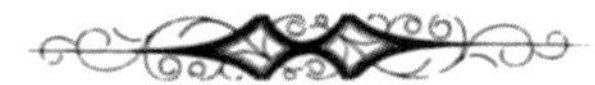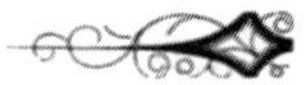

THE PRICE OF COAL

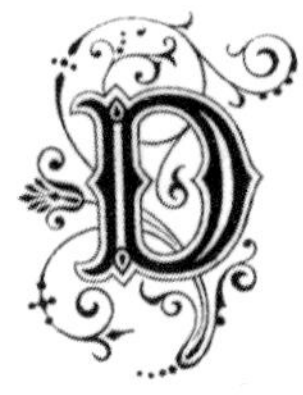uring the 19th century the loss of life in coal mines was a continuing blight on the industry; explosions were one of the commonest causes. Serious mining accidents throughout the country attracted national attention but smaller tragedies involving the loss of a few men were only reported locally, often on halfpenny broadsheets. In view of the national scale of the problem it seems strange that the great majority of accidents which are recorded on glass occurred in the North East. The reason is that glass making, as much as coal mining, was part of the North East tradition and glass, as well as being readily available, provided a surface that could easily be worked upon to provide a permanent record.

Compare this tradition with South Wales which was another major coal producing area but had no glass making. We have found no evidence that glass was ever used to commemorate mining accidents or other local events there. Pottery was an important manufacture in the area but did not appear to lend itself to an immediate and cheap response to minor tragedies in the same way that could be achieved by inscribing on glass. Because this story is intimately linked to the association of glassmaking and coalmining there is a brief account of the local history of each trade at the end of the book.

The mining-related glasses reveal stories of hardship, fortitude and courage that seem out of all proportion to what might have been expected of men working in difficult conditions for unreliable wages.

Only a small proportion of all the accidents that occurred in the North East seem to have been commemorated on glass and the majority of those that are recorded took place between

AN ACCOUNT OF THAT DREADFUL

EXPLOSION

WHICH TOOK PLACE AT

WEST MOOR COLLIERY,

On FRIDAY, October 31, 1851.

WHICH WAS ATTENDED WITH

LOSS OF LIFE.

We regret to have to record this day (Saturday), one of those fearful colliery accidents so fatal to

The following are the names of the unfortunate sufferers :—

1880-1916. The few examples we have recorded that pre-date this period all refer to accidents that fit the official definition of disasters, eg, Murton Colliery 1848 (2) and Washington 1851 (3) but we think it unlikely that the glasses were engraved at those dates.

After explosions, flooding and tunnel collapses were the most common causes of mining accidents but the most disastrous incident in the area, and the one that was almost certainly the most frequently commemorated on glass, was caused by freak circumstances that could never have been anticipated. It made national newspaper headlines, prompted a change in the law relating to coalmining and led to one of the biggest disaster funds ever collected.

HARTLEY COLLIERY

Hartley Colliery / Disaster Jany 16 1862 / 204 lives were lost

reverse with a fern (6)

The Hartley Colliery disaster on January 16, 1862 resulted in the loss of 204 lives. Most coal mines at that time had only one shaft giving access to the workings and in a large colliery this would be divided by wooden shuttering creating separate shafts to accommodate the cage on one side and the pumping and ventilation equipment on the other. At Hartley Colliery, as at many others, pumping was carried out by a steam-powered beam engine with the main beam extending over the shaft. The beam, weighing more than forty tons, suddenly failed and broke in two. One half fell into the mine, collapsing the shuttering and blocking the shaft

completely. The only chance of getting anybody out was to clear the wreckage, but it took many days to gain access and with no fresh air being pumped the result was inevitable. Five men who were ascending the shaft at the time were killed by the falling debris but 199 men and boys (and 43 pit ponies) died of

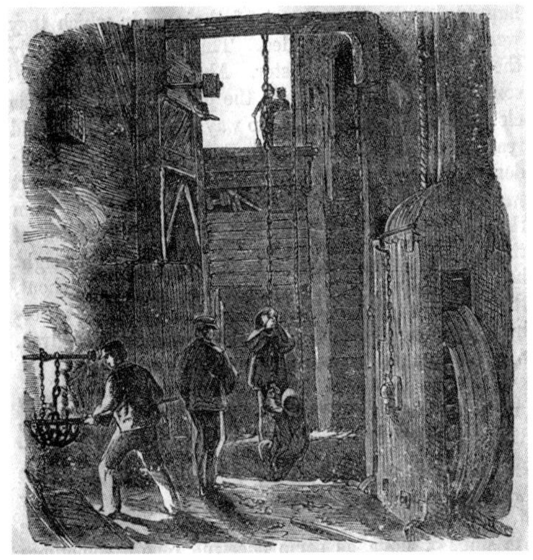

A graphic contemporary engraving.

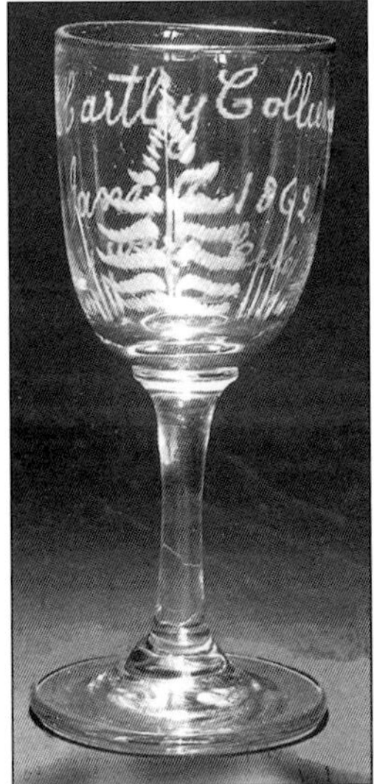

suffocation. As a result of the ensuing government enquiry, legislation was introduced that required all new mines to have two shafts. Half of the beam that caused the accident is still preserved in the Science Museum in London.

SACRISTON COLLIERY

Robert / Richardson / Rescued alive / after 91 hours / Peril

reverse with an unidentified plant flanked by ferns (25)

This inscription turned out to be connected with another glass bearing the legend *The Sacriston Disaster 3 miners entombed November 16th 1903*. Richardson was the only one of the three men who survived. His extraordinary rescue made national news and prompted an article in *Wide World Magazine*.

Two hundred men were working in the Busty seam when it was inundated by water that had burst through from an adjacent, abandoned part of the mine. Most managed to scramble to safety but three men were left trapped by the rising water. Of these, two drowned but Richardson was recovered alive after 91 hours. The rescue team was led by William C. Blackett who was, by all accounts, cast in the heroic mould of Victorian adventure story heroes. He was a mine agent, colliery engineer, explosives expert and a Captain in a Volunteer regiment. Although it was considered risky, he had a temporary dam erected to hold back the water, entered the mine and, as the water level dropped enough to provide some air, gradually managed to penetrate the shaft until he heard Richardson respond to his shouts.

Richardson, detached from his companions, found himself in an air pocket where he turned his coal tub upside down and, before his lamp went out, used it as a base to build a platform of planks to keep him clear of the water. He had lost track of time and given up hope when he heard the sound of his rescuer. Blackett remained underground for all but an hour of

SACRISTON COLLIERY DISASTER.

—

SUDDEN INRUSH OF WATER

—

FEARED LOSS OF THREE LIVES.

Newcastle Daily Journal, November 18, 1903

the time it took to rescue Richardson and was hailed as a hero. Recommended for the Silver medal of the Royal Humane Society, he was given the Gold. He went on to become a Colonel in the Territorial Army, commanded a regiment during the First World War, received an honorary degree from Durham University and became Deputy Lieutenant of Co. Durham in 1918.

This was not the only time he was involved in rescue operations and he kept a scrapbook of his exploits. In a long letter describing Richardson's rescue, he relates that when he found the miner alive he thought he was too weak to take soup so went all the way back to the surface to fetch him a flask of Bovril. It is perhaps a little strange that it was Richardson who was commemorated on glass when Blackett was the hero of the occasion. Perhaps a glass with his name upon it will come to light one day.

Kelloe Colliery

Kelloe Colliery / Disaster 6 May 1897 / 10 Lives lost.

reverse with diagonal fern (22)

Kelloe Colliery, also known as East Hetton Colliery, lies at Kelloe, south west of Durham City. In 1897 it was owned by Messrs Walter Scott & Company and was one of the largest mines in the district, employing over one thousand men underground. It was opened in 1836 and closed in 1983.

At about 3.30am on May 6, 1897, it was flooded by water bursting through from the adjacent disused Old Cassop Pit, fortunately before the foreshift had descended. There was some warning, but some of the victims may have died because they stopped to put on their clothes. Efforts were made to plug the defect by filling in the shaft of the Old Cassop mine. An old engine shed was demolished and tipped into the shaft together with large quantities of clay. Meanwhile the water was being pumped out. The rescue party, led by the manager, Mr Chipchase, was hindered by gas, but on May 11 they saw a deputy named Wilson, confused but wading through the water towards them. His first words were: 'My word, Master, I'm bonny glad to see you!' Finding his escape cut off by flooding and trapped in an area where there was three feet of water, he climbed on to some wooden beams until the water level subsided. Cold, hungry and disorientated, he thought that he had been trapped for about 24 hours but in fact it was more than four days. He made a good recovery and was back at work in three months.

This was the second disaster that Wilson had survived; he was the last person to be brought out alive following the explosion at Trimdon Grange pit in 1882.

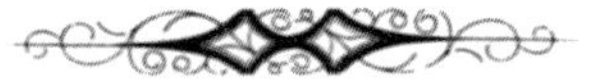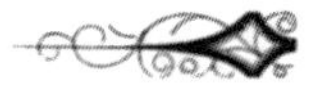

His trapped colleagues at Kelloe were not so lucky. Four bodies were recovered on May 12 and a further five on May 13 but it was not until May 26 that the tenth was brought to the surface. At the inquest the jury exonerated the company and the mining officials from any blame.

SEAHAM COLLIERY

Seaham Colliery / Explosion / 164 lives lost / Sept 8 1880 (7)

On Wednesday, September 8, 1880, while 231 men and boys were underground at Seaham, a small group of men was enlarging refuge holes in the curved roadway between the two shafts. (Refuge holes are cut in the sides of roads to allow men to stand aside from passing tubs). At about 2.20am, a shot was fired at the curve and the pit exploded with such force that it was heard at Murton Colliery, a mile and a half away. 164 men perished, some in the first blast. but the majority died from carbon monoxide poisoning when afterdamp spread slowly through the pit. The explosion was

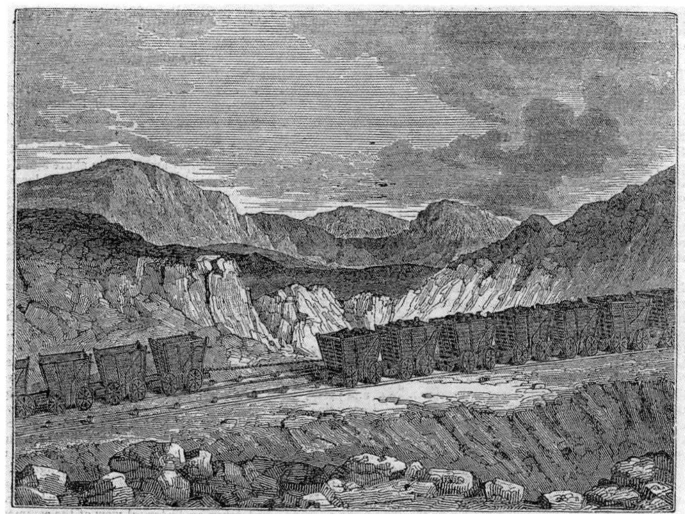

Seaham Colliery depicted in the Penny Magazine.

heard at both the High and Low pitheads and the ground shook, waking people in the village and bringing crowds to the scene. The shaft and cage had been damaged and tons of debris had to be cleared before rescuers could descend on ropes. At the Maudlin seam all the ponies had suffocated and further through the seam rescuers found mutilated bodies and debris. One week later the team located George Dixon, a shifter who had been entombed. He told them that a driver-boy lay injured with him and could not move. Two days later rescuers broke through and found the child clasped in the shifter's arms. Both were dead.

When the body of Michael Smith was brought back to his wife she found a tin water bottle under his arm. On it he had scratched, at different times: 'Dear Margaret, There was forty of us altogether at 7am. Some was singing hymns, but my thoughts were on my little Michael. I thought that he and l would meet in heaven at the same time. Oh dear wife God save you and the children, and pray for myself, Dear Wife, farewell, my last thoughts bout you and the children. Be sure and learn them to pray for me; Oh what an awfull position we are in'.

Michael's son was ill when he left for work and died on the day of the explosion.

BARRINGTON COLLIERY

An Alarming / Accident Occurred / at / Barrington Colliery / 13 July 1894

reverse with a clover leaf (15)

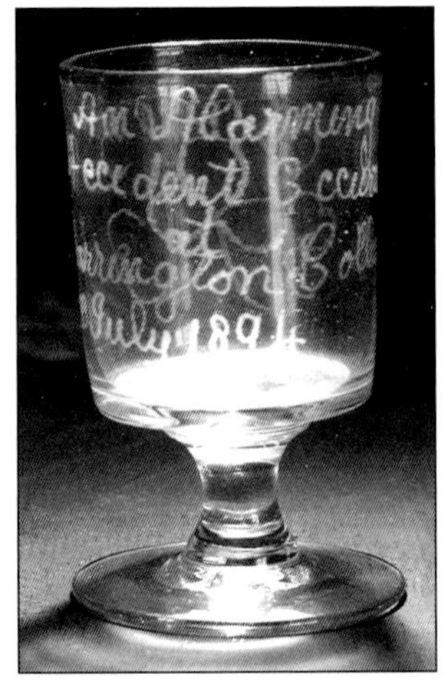

This glass is unusual as it records an accident involving equipment but no loss of life. Just before a shift change one of the coal tubs had not been fully loaded into the cage when the winding gear was put in motion. The tub caught on the side of the shaft and did such damage that it was impossible to bring the men to the surface. The cage was broken and had to be replaced. As a result the men could not be rescued until the following day. As *The Newcastle Daily Journal* reported, 'the accident did not occasion any injury to life or limb, yet the damage will be very considerable to the owners, the Bedlington Coal Company'.

NORTH SEATON COLLIERY

In Memory of / Edward Wilson / who was killed at / North Seaton / 16 Nov 1894 aged 23

reverse with *Remember Me* and a clover leaf (17)

Four men were travelling on a flat trolley to begin work at the coal face when a large rock fell from the side wall and crushed the two in the middle (Edward Wilson and Philip Grieves). Wilson's right knee and thigh were severely crushed while Grieves' left foot was injured as well as his head and back. The overmen gave first aid, stemming the flow of blood and amputating one of Grieves' toes which hung by a thread.

When Wilson was carried home the doctor amputated his leg at the hip but the miner died

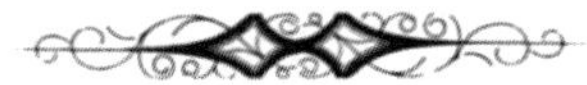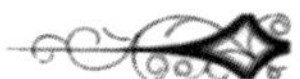

shortly afterwards. Even today, with skilled anaesthesia, blood transfusion and asepsis, amputation at the hip is a major operation. It is not surprising that poor Edward Wilson did not survive.

NEW DELAVAL

In Memory of/ John George Whitlock / Who was accidentally Killed / at New Dalaval (sic) *Colliery / 8 April 1895 / Age 13 years 11 months*

reverse with fern and *Gone But Not Forgotten* (18)

Children regularly worked underground but it is unusual to find someone as young as this commemorated on a glass. This tragedy is briefly reported in the *Morpeth Herald* for April 13, 1895.

The inquest was held at the Percy Arms Inn, Kitty Brewster. According to James Tanny, of Cowpen Village the accident occurred about 10am.

He and 'some of his marrows'*, were at work when they heard a set coming behind them, 'going faster than he ought to have gone'. They stepped aside to let it pass, and almost immediately they heard a crash as though the tub had 'got off the way' and a groan. The tub had left the way and young John was lying' across the limmers'**. Blood had 'gushed from his nostrils' and he was 'quite dead'.

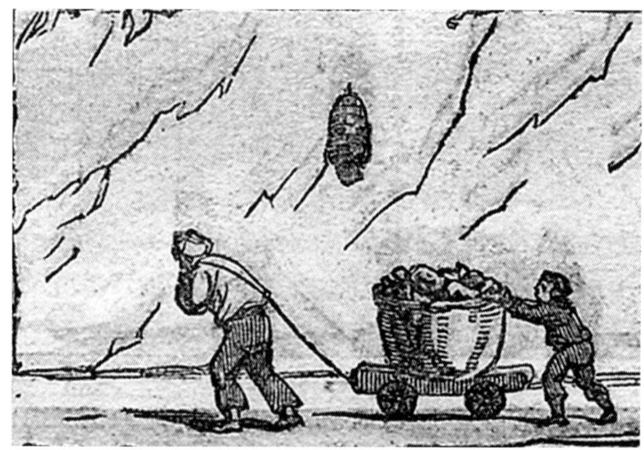

From Matthias Dunn's 'Winning and Working of Collieries', 1849.

* A 'marrow' (pronounced and sometimes written marra) is a workmate, doing the same job and sharing the same paynote.

** Actually limber but pronounced limmer (and spelled as such in the newspaper report). A limber was made up of two wooden shafts connected by an iron bow to a hinged hook for connection to a tub. Limbers were permanently fastened to the pony during its working shift.

USWORTH COLLIERY

In Memory of / Usworth Colliery / Explosion March 2nd / 1885

reverse fern (9)

Usworth village lies just north of Washington and east of Springwell, County Durham. The colliery was sunk about 1845 and in 1885 was owned by John Bowes Esq. & Partners. There were two main shafts, Wellington East and West, divided by bratticing, and a back shaft by which the uninjured men were brought to the surface. The seams of coal worked were the Maudlin, the Low Main (where the explosion occurred) and the Hutton, one of the deepest in the county. About 600 men and boys were employed, producing 1,000 tons of coal a day. The colliery worked a two shift system; the back-shift men came out at about 5pm and the night-shift men were due to go down at 9pm. In the interval the 4 pm shift went down to prepare the workings for the night-shift. At the time of the accident on Monday, March 2, there were fewer men in the mine than at any other time of day.

The first batch of night-shift men was stepping into the cage when there was a loud report, followed by a cloud of dust rushing up the shaft. Everyone knew there had been an explosion and soon a crowd gathered at the pit. The West shaft was blocked so there was very little hope of reaching the trapped miners in time to save their lives. Between 30 and 35 people were in the East Pit and 45 in the West Pit where the explosion had occurred. Although the West shaft was blocked, it was possible to bring men in the East pit safely to the surface. Soon after entering the pit, three of the rescue party were overcome by afterdamp. One managed to return to the surface in a semi-conscious state but both his companions perished. Clearing the blocked West shaft proceeded with difficulty; meanwhile the colliery carpenters were making coffins. By midnight on Tuesday, March 3, rescuers had only been able to penetrate about 400 yards from the shaft. At 8am on Wednesday the first body was found. Including the two members of the rescue party, 42 men and boys (and 72 ponies) died in the disaster.

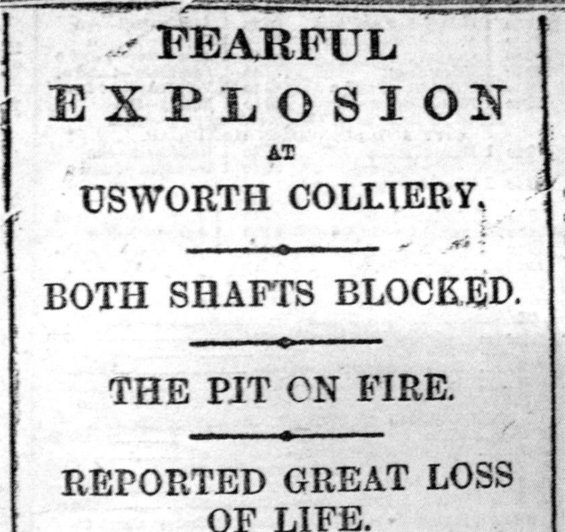

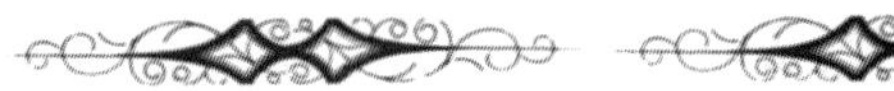

We have recorded three further glasses relating to this disaster:

*A present to Barbara Meek From her Mother Usworth Colliery Explosion
March 2nd 1885*

Mrs. Night / Usworth Colliery Explosion / March 2nd 1885

J.J. Gordon / Usworth Colliery / Explosion March 2nd /1885

Who were Barbara Meek, Mrs Night and J.J. Gordon? The detailed newspaper accounts record the names of all the dead and injured as well as numerous mining and Union officials, rescuers, doctors and others who 'assisted in the operations', but none match the above.

An earlier accident at Usworth is referred to on the following glass.

*John Graham / Who Died March 29th 1885 / Through an Accident at /
Usworth Colliery / Nov 28th 1884*

We can find no public report of any accident on that day or of the death of John Graham. The death certificate issued by Dr James Gardner states that Graham died of acute rheumatism and double pneumonia; that is, natural causes. No accident is mentioned. John Graham is, however, mentioned in the Usworth Colliery Miners' Union Minute books as dying six months after being involved in an accident in 1884. The cause of his death was important for the family since had they proved his death was due to his employment they might have claimed compensation. The inscriptions appear to be trying to make a point.

The pit would experience another three deaths in 1891.

*In memory of / William Bell / Who. lost. his. life / By. an. Boiler Explosion / At.
Usworth. Colliery / April. 11 1891 / Aged. 23. Years* (13)

Poor William Bell was one of three who died when a boiler used for raising steam to the underground hauling engines blew up soon after noon on Saturday April 11. The explosion was heard and felt at the surface, and heavy battens and cement were hurled into the air. The inquest found the boiler plate had deteriorated to the point of danger (from half an inch to an eighth of an inch thick), and should have been reported as unsafe long before. Though there was some dispute about entries in the boiler book, blame was laid at the door of the foreman enginewright, Robert Wraith, and George Elwen, engineer, who had examined the boiler a fortnight before but concluded the thinning metal at the waterline 'would last the time out'. William Bell, who died of scalds and burns was cleared of any blame, as was the Manager, Mr Stokoe, who denied having been informed of the deteriorating boiler.

BEBSIDE COLLIERY

Bebside Disaster / 15 July 1905 (26)

A number of deputies and a small group of men were working during the holidays under the direction of the manager, Mr Davis, to extend the overhead pulley system used to drag the coal tubs along the rails. They had installed a new pulley on a curve in the tunnel. Though all appeared satisfactory at first, the rope became detached and jammed in the sheave. With the winding engine still running the pulley was torn out of the roof, bringing down timber and iron beams. Two of the men were buried and killed immediately. A third was trapped but was recovered alive although he died shortly afterwards.

WEST STANLEY

West Stanley / Disaster / 168 lives lost / Feby 16 1909 (34)

This was another accident that led to a change to the laws controlling coalmining. An explosion occurred at 3.45 pm on February 16, 1909, followed barely a minute later by an even larger one. By 27 February 166 bodies had been recovered and the search for the last two was called off. The mass funeral was attended by enormous crowds with one report stating that 11,000 mourners had arrived by train. The dead were buried in mass graves and the graveside burial services lasted five hours. The bodies of the two men unaccounted for at the time were finally discovered, 34 years later, in March 1933.

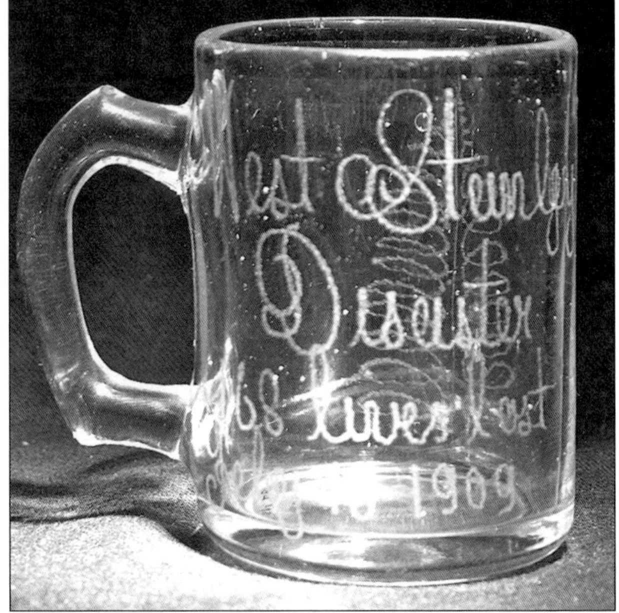

It is likely that the first explosion was caused by firedamp and the second by coal dust. As a result of the enquiry that followed, men were required to carry two numbered tokens; one to be handed in when they went down the pit and another to hand in when they re-surfaced.

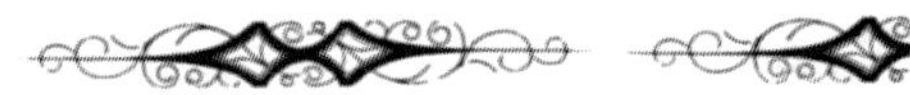

In 1995, a memorial at the site of the pit, which closed in 1936, was dedicated by footballer Kevin Keegan, whose grandfather was a member of the rescue team.

THREE MEN RESCUED ALIVE.

A Shorter Death Roll now Expected.

An optimistic headline in the Newcastle Daily Journal on February 17, 1909.

WOODHORN COLLIERY

WOODHORN DISASTER / Aug 13 1916 13 LIVES LOST (39)

This is the most recent accident recorded on a glass that we have found so far and it is the only one with the inscription entirely in upper case characters. A party of 30 men was engaged in maintenance on a Sunday, erecting steel girders. It is probable that one of them took a naked flame into an area where there had been a build up of gas. There was an explosion which killed 11 miners instantly. Another two were recovered but died later.

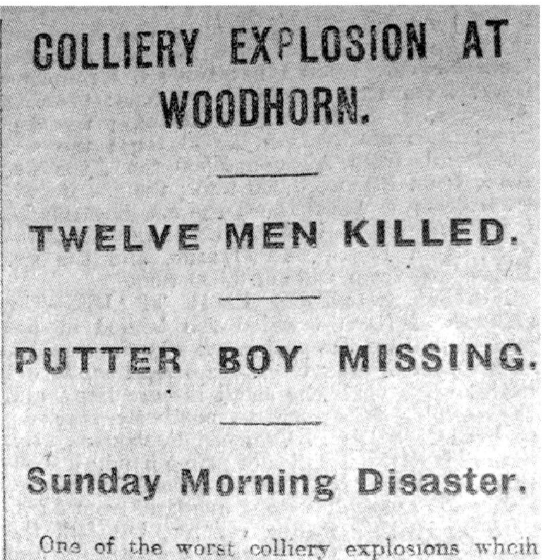

COLLIERY EXPLOSION AT WOODHORN.

TWELVE MEN KILLED.

PUTTER BOY MISSING.

Sunday Morning Disaster.

One of the worst colliery explosions whcih

Newcastle Daily Chronicle.

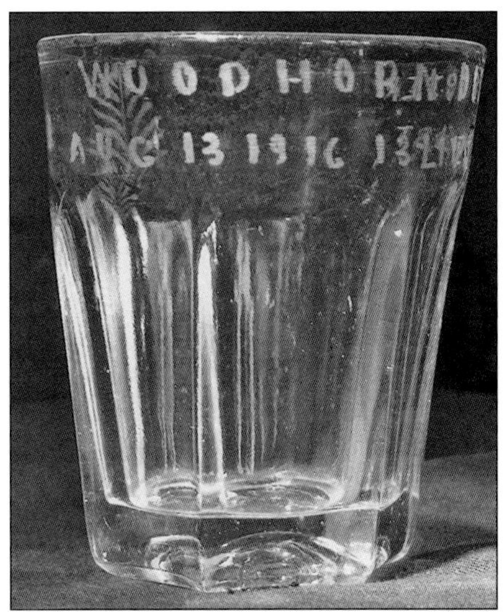

WHITBURN COLLIERY

Whitburn Colliery / Mystery Solved / Overseers Body Found /1907 (30)

Daniel Mark Bence, aged 45, was a back-overman (a shift foreman) at the pit. He left his house for work on the morning of April 2, apparently quite well. The overman in charge met Bence in the stables and after getting the ponies out, they went in-bye together. After about a mile the overman gave Bence directions for his round. Bence set off around 8 am, saying that he would return by the same road. He should have finished his whole round by noon. When he did not return a search party was mounted but no trace of him was found despite systematic searching.

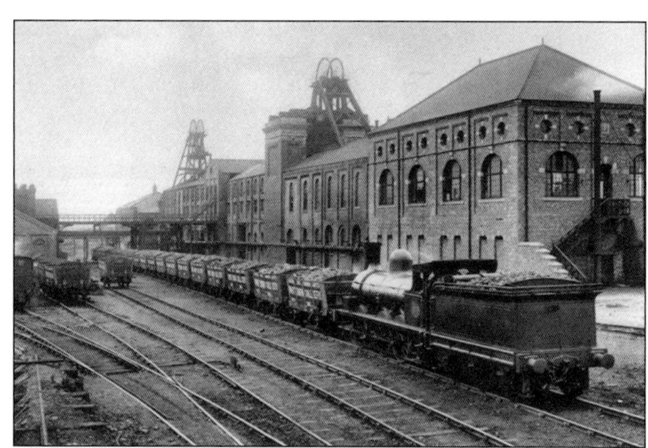

Whitburn Colliery in the 1890s.

On the morning of May 7 the smell of a decomposing body was noticed in a disused working about a mile from the shaft, in the opposite direction to that in which Bence had intended to go. Bence was lying on his back with arms folded, trapped behind a fall of stone. The area in which he was found was between two and three feet high. Bence's lamp was found 35 yards away from the body

At autopsy doctors agreed that the external injuries to the body had been sustained after death. The colliery doctor, who had known Bence said the victim had lost a lot of weight. The conclusion was that Bence had died of starvation. The coroner asked whether Bence 'might have suddenly lost his mind whilst wandering about' and the doctor replied: 'I think he would be a man who would be liable to lose his presence of mind from what I know of him'.

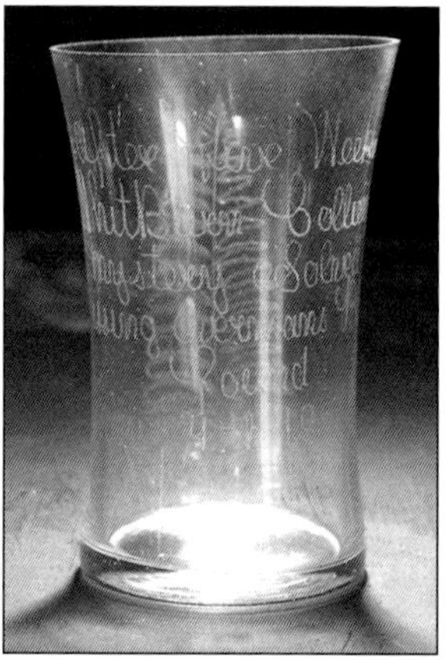

How, and for what purpose Bence had got into the old workings, we will never know.

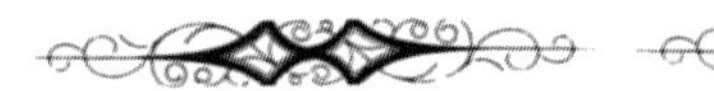

The following glasses record other matters concerning the mining community.

The Strike / of Durham Miners / april 5th 1844

reverse with a diagonal fern (40)

In Durham, miners were tied to the mine owner by a legally enforceable agreement known as the bond. Miners signed, or in many cases put their marks to, the bond once a year on the binding day. The terms of the bond were harsh and included penalties that often meant that miners, after working a full shift could be in debt to the owners. In March 1844, 20,000 pitmen from Northumberland and Durham met and agreed that they would not sign the owner's bond but only a bond acceptable to them and drawn up by William P. Roberts, the legal representative of the Miners' Association of Great Britain. This was the start of the first combined strike of Northumberland and Durham miners.

All collieries agreed to stay out pending a universal agreement. There was some violence in the early days of the strike; at South Hetton 20 hewers and deputies had signed the bond before the strike began and on April 5 their houses were attacked and windows smashed. By May Lord Londonderry's coal stocks were nearly exhausted. Meeting pitmen at Penshaw he told them to 'return to work or make way for those who will.' He then began evictions at Pittington and Rainton, introducing labour from his Irish estates. During June more blacklegs from Wales, Staffordshire, Cornwall and Ireland were brought in and more families were evicted; small tented encampments appeared

STRIKE OF THE COLLIERS.
AGGREGATE MEETING ON BLACK FELL, DURHAM.

An immense gathering of the miners of Northumberland and Durham was held on Black Fell, near Gateshead, on Monday, to determine upon the course to be adopted with regard to the differences which at present exist between them and the coal-owners. It was calculated that men belonging to 130 collieries were on the ground, forming, with others more or less remotely connected with the mining interest, an aggregate of not less than 20,000 persons. Thousands of these had travelled on foot from the most distant parts of both counties. Most of the groups carried with them gaily-decorated banners, bearing appropriate mottoes, and not a few were accompanied with bands of music. As each took up its position on the hill, and the men threw themselves on the turf for refreshment or repose, the scene became both animating and picturesque—effects which were greatly aided by the brilliancy of the day, and detracted from only by the serious, perhaps painful, associations with which the circumstances were connected.

Newcastle Courant reports the strike meeting in 1844.

along hedgerows and on the moors. Although the strike remained relatively solid until the end of July, hardship and blacklegs weakened the will to continue and after 240 families from Flintshire were settled in the Hetton and Lambton pits in August, over 100 union men, mainly in Durham, returned to work. By the end of August it was all over.

(Whether or not this glass is contemporary with the event recorded is discussed on page 60.)

Better Luck / To the Durham Miners / 1894

reverse with clover leaf (43)

We have also recorded another version of this inscription, *Better Luck / to the Northumberland Miners / 1894* (44) and there may be a connection between these and the glass that follows.

In 1893 the coal trade was in recession. The minutes of the Northumberland Miners' Mutual Confident Association record that on January 28 they met coal owners at the Coal Trade Office to consider a reduction of wages. Small coal was almost unsaleable and prices were still falling. Depression of shipping had reduced the demand for steam coal. The owners felt that 'the condition of trade' compelled them to ask for a reduction of 7.5%. Wages in Fife had been reduced by 25% and in South Wales by 35%. The Association committee advised the miners to accept a reduction of 5%, but the workers voted against this. Throughout the country men at collieries connected with the Miners' Federation, including those in Durham, (but not Northumberland), came out on strike demanding an increase in pay but all these actions failed. Northumberland miners reaped a temporary reward of a small rise in pay in September, reflecting an improvement in the price of coal.

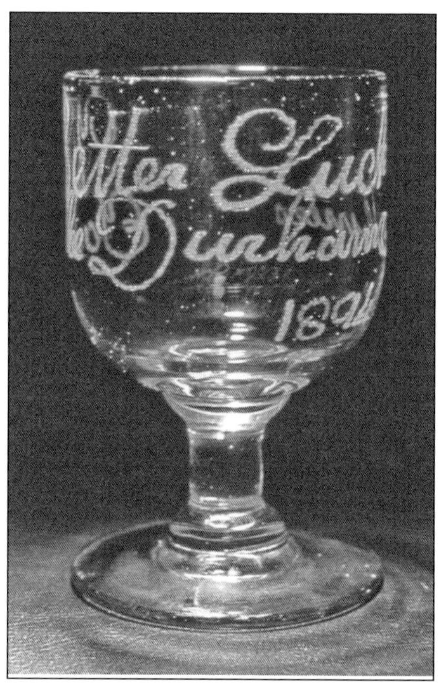

Deborah Moffat, of Woodhorn Museum has suggested that, so bad had the prospects for coalmining been in 1893, that these 'Better Luck' glasses were probably engraved in early 1894 as tokens of hope for the New Year.

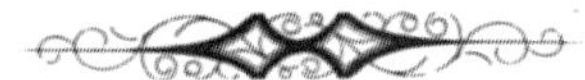 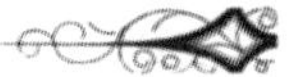

Northumberland Miners / Advance of 7¹⁄₂ Per Cent / January 13 1894

reverse with a clover leaf) (45)

At a meeting on Saturday January 13 at the Coal Trade Office, Newcastle upon Tyne, the agents of the Northumberland miners applied for an increase in their wages. The owners had previously granted a provisional advance of 5% to be paid by six fortnightly pay days. Following a long discussion the owners agreed to increase this to 7.5% to be paid with effect from the next pay day.

The Memorial Stone / Of a New Miners Hall / Was laid at / Ashington Colliery / 6 Sept 1894

reverse with a diagonal fern (47)

The Miners' Mutual Benefit Society for Northumberland involved itself in all matters relating to the employment of miners, disagreements with employers and the general welfare of the

mining community. It made a loan of £3000 towards the building of Ashington Miners' Hall. The scheme ran into trouble because the committee considered that the 14 inch walls of the new hall were not thick enough in relation to the proposed height of the building, but eventually disagreements were resolved to everyone's satisfaction and the money was finally paid to Ashington on March 16, 1895, six months after the foundation stone had been laid.

It is not immediately apparent why such mundane events were remembered in this fashion. We know that glasses were presented as mementoes to those involved in specific events as demonstrated by those presented to members of a Mine Rescue Brigade (page 59). Could those that refer to wage increases have been produced as souvenirs for the Union members who negotiated the increase? Did the managing committee who oversaw the building of the new Ashington Miners' Hall in 1894 or all the people present at the stone laying ceremony receive a glass as a memento?

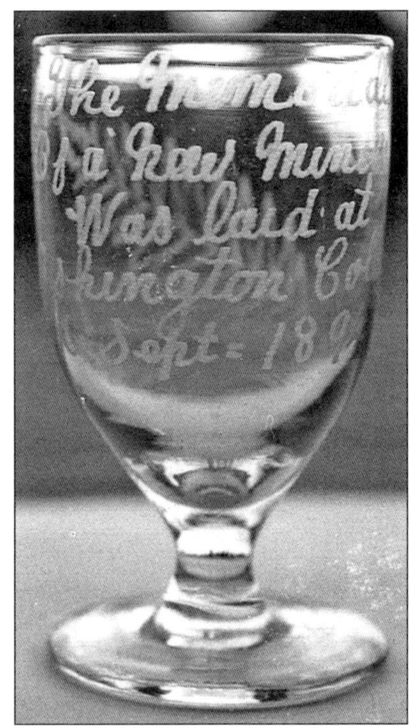

SAD TIDINGS

his group of glasses records fatal accidents that occurred locally involving anything from one individual to 200. While other national disasters such as the sinking of the *Titanic* are discussed in a later chapter, the following records appear to be peculiar to glasses produced in the North East.

Victoria Hall / Disaster June 16 1883 / 200 children lost there [sic] *lives.*

reverse three-petalled flower on stem with two small leaves (58)

At the Victoria Hall in Sunderland on June 16, 1883, there was a show for children at which prizes and presents were promised. About 2,000 children, but few adults, were present and

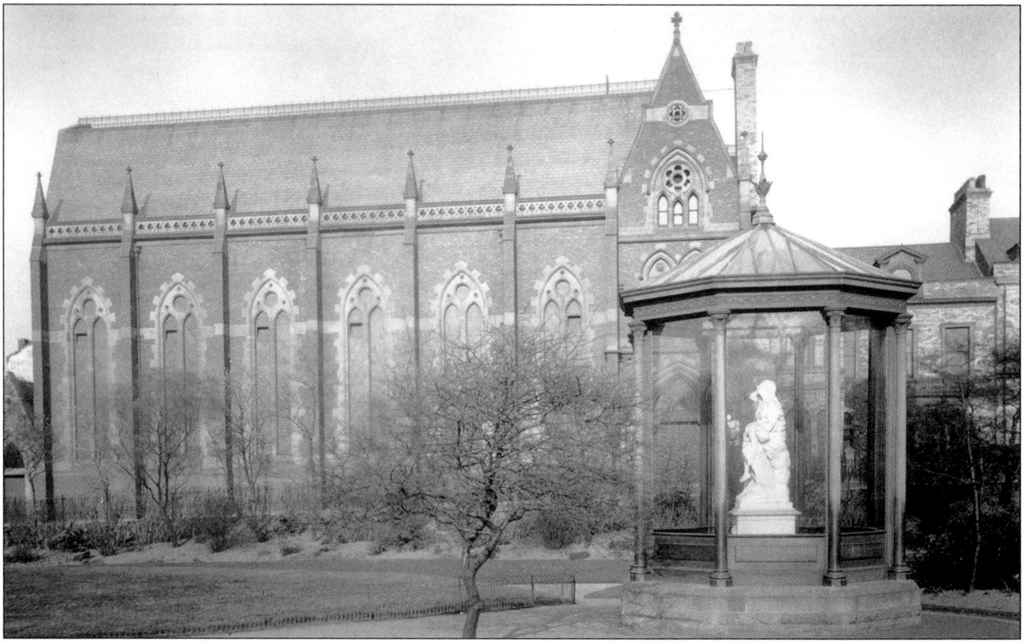

Victoria Hall and the statue to the memory of the disaster, in the 1890s.

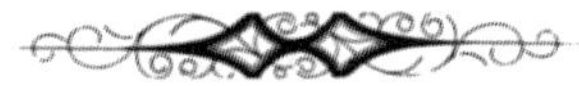
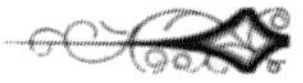

when the time arrived for the gifts to be distributed there was a rush of children from the gallery to get to the stage. Their progress was blocked by an inward-opening swing door at the bottom of the staircase from the gallery. It was bolted to the floor before the performance to control the flow of people to the box office and nobody had raised the bolt to allow it to open freely. In the resulting melée nearly 400 children were trapped behind the door. After lifting out 200 alive, the rescuers found the bodies of 183 crushed and suffocated victims. Donations to a relief fund came from all over the country, including £50 from Queen Victoria.

The number of deaths recorded on the glasses commemorating this tragedy varies from 182 to 200. One explanation might be that in the rush to produce glasses the engraver relied on an estimate of the number of deaths. The figure would be amended as the actual death toll was established. If this were so it may be a clue to the motives of those who produced the glasses.

In response to the disaster new legislation required all places of public entertainment to have adequate access with all doors opening outwards. A white marble statue of a mother cradling her dead child was erected in Sunderland's Mowbray Park but in the 1930s, vandalised and considered too sombre, it was moved to a cemetery. In 2002 183 children took part in a re-dedication ceremony when the restored memorial was re-erected in the park, a short distance from the site of Victoria Hall.

S.S. Regian Wrecked Upon the Bondicar Rock Between Broomhill and Amble 1884 (75)

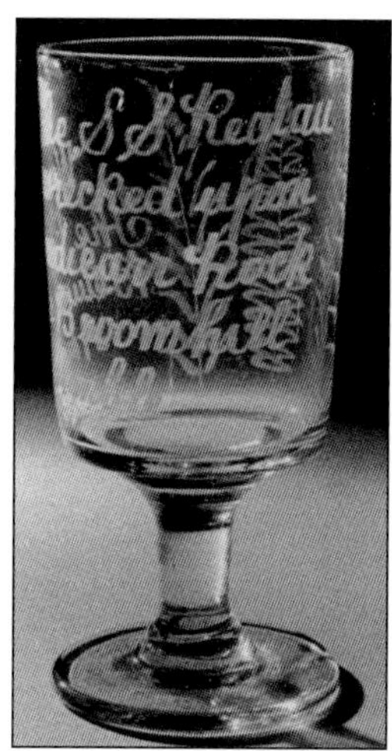

The SS *Regian*, under the command of Captain Stodart, was a barquentine-rigged steamer, registered in Liverpool, on its way from Calcutta to Dundee with a cargo of jute.

At six o'clock on the evening of November 5, 1884, the ship ran aground on rocks about two miles south of Coquet Island. *Newcastle Daily Journal* refers to them as Hadson Skeers rather than Bondicar Rock. Five feet of water flooded 'the second compartment' and part of the cargo was jettisoned. The crew, numbering 33 hands, was taken off 'by rocket apparatus' according to one report. At any rate, the Hauxley lifeboat landed some members of the crew and the remainder were put on board the tug *Pactolus* by the ship's boat. They were brought to the Harbour Inn in Amble.

There were some hopes that a part of the cargo could be saved, albeit damaged, but the vessel was a total wreck.

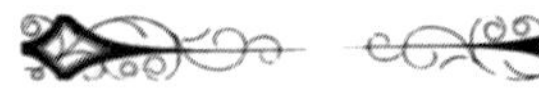
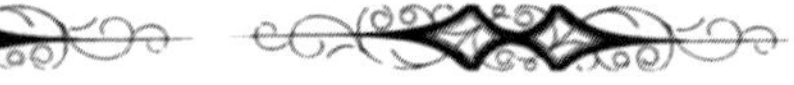

In the years 1860-1910 594 ships were wrecked on the coasts of Northumberland and Durham. Why, then, was the relatively unremarkable wrecking of the SS *Regian* singled out for commemoration? The production of glasses could hardly be to raise money for dependents or relatives since no loss of life was recorded and the ship was not even registered locally.

In Memory of John Paterson Connell 22 July 1880 Quality Row, Cambois (57)

Connell was employed as a joiner at Cambois Colliery. One hot day he went to the beach to bathe. He was sweating and the shock of the cold water is thought to have caused a cramp; observers saw him having difficulty in the water. John Crawford went to his aid but a strong undertow had already sucked the unfortunate Connell down. Crawford dived under and managed to pull him up by his hair but all efforts to revive him failed. His body was then carried to his parents' house in Quality Row.

In Memory of John Henry Todd / Who was Drowned / on the 4th July 1894 / at Blyth aged 23 years

reverse with clover (59)

Neither Todd nor the companions he was with could swim but they went into the water on a strong ebb tide. Two variants of this inscription have come to our notice which raise questions about how and why the glasses were produced. One gives his age but omits the reference to Blyth. The other includes Blyth but omits his age. Variations would be likely when large numbers of glasses by more than one engraver were produced for a major disaster or a national event, but glasses to commemorate

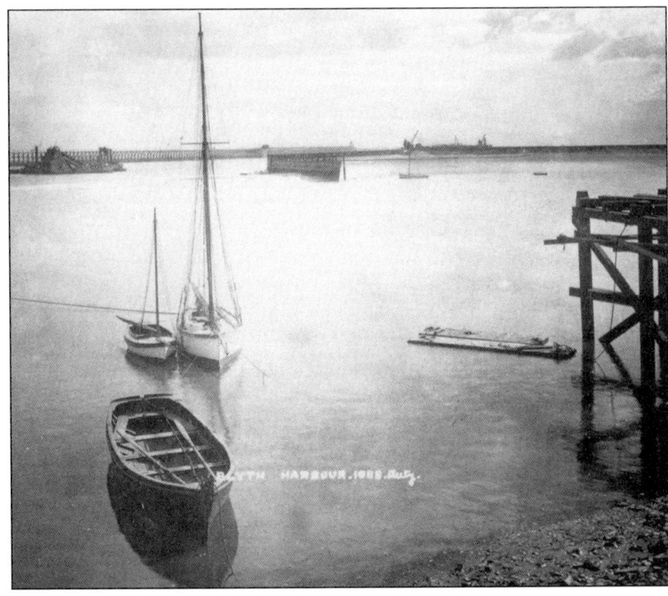

Blyth harbour around 1890.

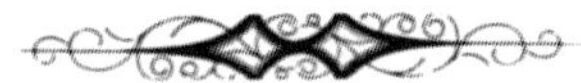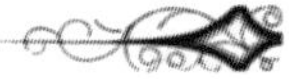

an individual, even though he may have been well known and highly regarded, can only have been produced in limited quantities for distribution, sale or presentation in quite a small area. There are several possible explanations. Some may have been commissioned specifically for presentation to family members at the funeral. Others may have been commissioned by individuals or friends outside the family. They may have been produced by more than one engraver or not all produced at the same time. Or they may have been produced by the same engraver who varied the inscription according to whim.

This is not the only example of several glasses relating to a single event having variations in the inscription. See the Newbiggin disaster below.

In memory of four Blyth men / George W. Nicholson 22 / George Brown 30 / Thomas Brown 21 / George Dawson 30 / who were drowned 13 July 1895

reverse yacht between vertical ferns (61)

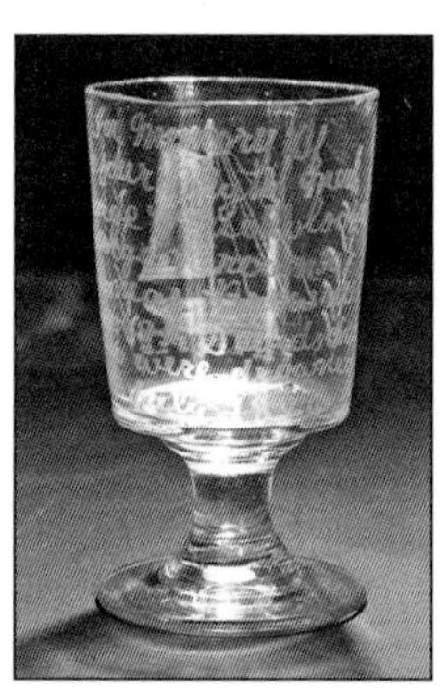

One Saturday afternoon these four men left Blyth in the *Marie*, a small sailing boat, for what was probably a pleasure cruise. George Brown, a seaman for some 15 years, was considered to be an expert sailor. None of the men were believed to be swimmers.

The weather was described as 'rather rough' on the Saturday and 'pretty rough' on Sunday and when they had not returned a yacht set out to look for them. It was hoped that they might have found shelter in another harbour somewhere along the coast but a telegram was received on Monday to say that a steamer had passed a boat, bottom up, off Blyth that fitted the description of the *Marie*.

New Biggin Disaster / Dec 9th 1904 / Seven Fisherman (sic) Lost (63)

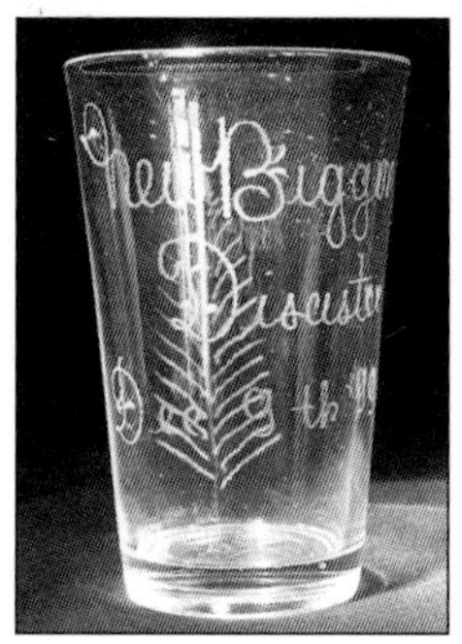

Most of the other glasses that we have seen recording this accident omit the number of deaths. The steamship *Anglia* travelling from Norway to Sunderland ran aground on the Needle's Eye Rocks. The alarm gun was fired and the lifeboat was launched, and several cobles manned by local fishermen set off to see if there was any opportunity for salvage. One of them, manned by eight men, seven of them members of the Armstrong family, reached the stricken ship and were discussing salvage with the captain when a large wave capsized the boat. The lifeboat immediately went to the spot but only one man,

John Armstrong, was recovered.

At the enquiry into the disaster Armstrong said that the sea was bitterly cold, the swell was extremely heavy so that his companions were repeatedly washed off the upturned hull of their boat and none of them could swim. The bodies were later recovered and thousands attended the mass funeral. A public disaster fund was opened in Newcastle on the December 13. Ironically the 17 members of the *Anglia*'s crew were rescued later the same day.

In Loving Memory / of Lady Grey / Wife of Sir Edward Grey / Who died as the result of / a Trap accident / Near Alnwick / February 4th 1906

reverse *In the Midst of Life we are in Death* (66)

We have recorded this inscription on a large jug in Beamish Museum and on several small tankards in private collections. In all cases the engraving is better than average, possibly because it relates to someone of high social standing, highly regarded in the area.

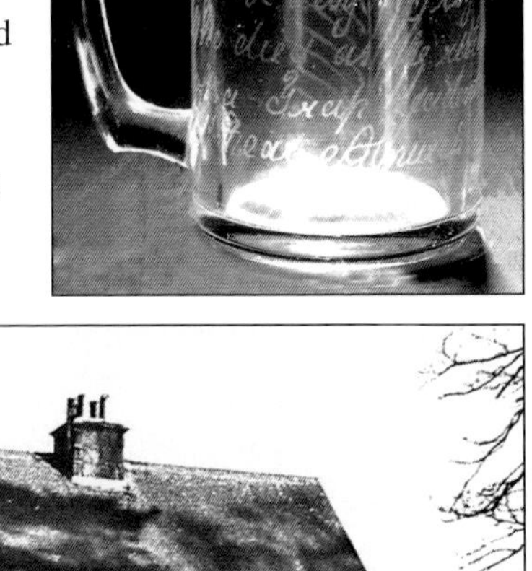

On the afternoon of Thursday February 1, 1906, Lady Dorothy Grey, aged 41 and the wife of Sir Edward Grey, the Foreign Minister, was flung from her trap, and sustained head injuries from which she died on February 4.

At the inquest Thomas Henderson, under gardener at Fallodon, the Greys' home, was asked 'Was the horse a quiet one?' He replied: 'Well, it had been prancing several times'. About 50 or 60 yards south of Ellingham school house, with Lady Grey driving, the horse suddenly shied to the left, the left wheel struck a stump in the hedge and the cart overturned. The horse may have been frightened by a heap of scaffolding poles lying close to the road. Lady Grey and Henderson were both thrown to the ground. She was conveyed to the school house where Dr Watson, who arrived 45 minutes later, found her on a sofa, unconscious and bleeding from the ear. He diagnosed fracture of the base of the skull and consulted Dr Rutherford

The Ellingham school house.

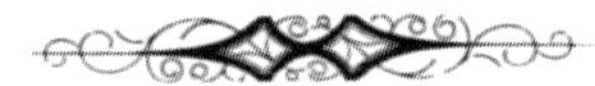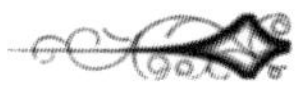

Morison of Newcastle and 'other medical gentlemen'. Lady Grey died in the schoolhouse without regaining consciousness.

Lady Grey's body was taken by special train to be cremated at Darlington then her ashes were taken back to Ellingham. Darlington was the nearest crematorium to her home at Fallodon in Northumberland and only the fifth one to open in England. There was no crematorium in Newcastle upon Tyne until 1934. Cremation was unusual in 1906 and Lady Grey was ahead of her time. There were memorial services at Embleton parish church and at St Margaret's, Westminster.

The following two glasses refer to coal mines and appear, at first sight, to be related to mining accidents but on investigation this proves not to be the case.

In Memory of / John & Thomas William Nobley / Who Were Drowned at / Barrington Colliery Jan 9 1895 / Age 11 & 8 Years

reverse *O Think of The / home over there* (60)

This glass was to be the inspiration for the writing of this book.

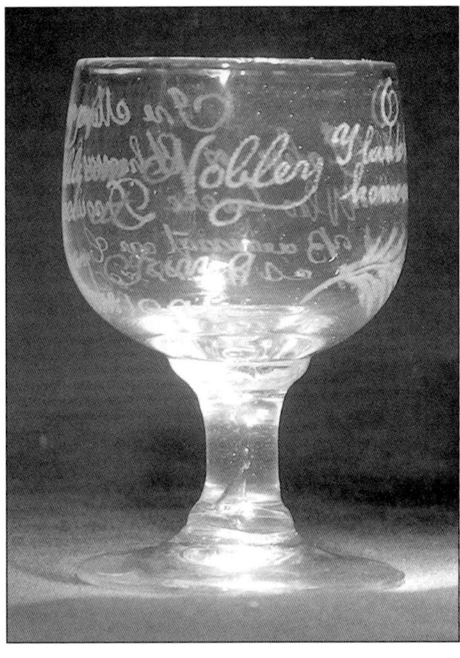

The connection with Barrington Colliery is only incidental as the article in the *Newcastle Daily Journal* for January 11 makes clear. 'On Wednesday afternoon two brothers aged 7 & 11, the sons of Mr John Noble, miner, Barrington Colliery near Choppington were skating on a reservoir belonging to the colliery when suddenly the ice gave way and both were precipitated into the water which is some fourteen feet deep. An alarm was raised, the father of the lads being among those who first arrived to render assistance. Noble, anxious about his boys rushed into the water followed by Mr Blandford, another employee at the colliery. After some searching the father brought the lifeless body of one of the boys to the surface, the other body being recovered about an hour after. Mr Noble was himself very much exhausted and it was with difficulty that he was rescued.'

This tragedy is frequently recorded on glass but you will notice that the age of one brother and the spelling of the surname on the inscription is different from that given in the newspaper. More recently we have seen a glass on which the name has been inscribed as 'Noble' and we presume that this version must have used the newspaper report as its source. The birth and death certificates confirm that the family name was, in fact, Nobley.

A Serious Fire Ashington Colliery on Saturday 19 Oct 1895. Accidents will happen.

reverse, a fern (49)

At first sight this glass suggested a pit accident since fires below ground were a regular occurrence. On investigation we discovered that it concerned a house fire. According to the *Morpeth Herald and Reporter* fire broke out, a little after 8pm, at the home of Walter Elliott in Fifth Row, Ashington Colliery. Mrs Elliott had been ill in bed for a considerable time, and although Mr Elliott had stayed with her almost constantly, he left the house for a short time that day and returned to find it in flames and his wife crawling naked towards the door. He ran inside, wrapped her in a blanket and carried her to a neighbour while flames spread to the adjoining cottages. A large crowd of horrified people assembled and messengers were sent to the Colliery officials, but, as it was pay Saturday, many were not at home. The manual fire engine was set to work, by which time several houses were 'well alight'. The pump became choked so they tried other methods of stopping the fire. Gaps were cut through the roofs of houses on either side of the fire and the hose was coupled to water pipes in the locomotive shed. The pipe was about 100 yards too short but this was made up with lengths of 2 inch piping 'which brought a copious supply of water under good pressure to bear upon the flames'.

At one point it was thought that the entire row of houses would be consumed and householders began to remove their furniture, but by midnight the fire was under control. Those families who had lost their homes stayed with friends, leaving furniture in gardens. Seven houses were totally destroyed.

There would almost certainly have been an open fire in Mrs Elliott's bedroom and it was once common practice to light the upstairs fire with a shovelful of burning coals taken from the downstairs fire. The possibilities for an accident are obvious.

No lives were lost but there were a number of minor injuries and in one or two instances families lost nearly all their furniture. 'In a few cases it is alleged that downright plundering was engaged in by a section of vicious miscreants' who, while other people were distracted by the fire, made off with furniture that had been left outside for safety. Shortly before 10pm a

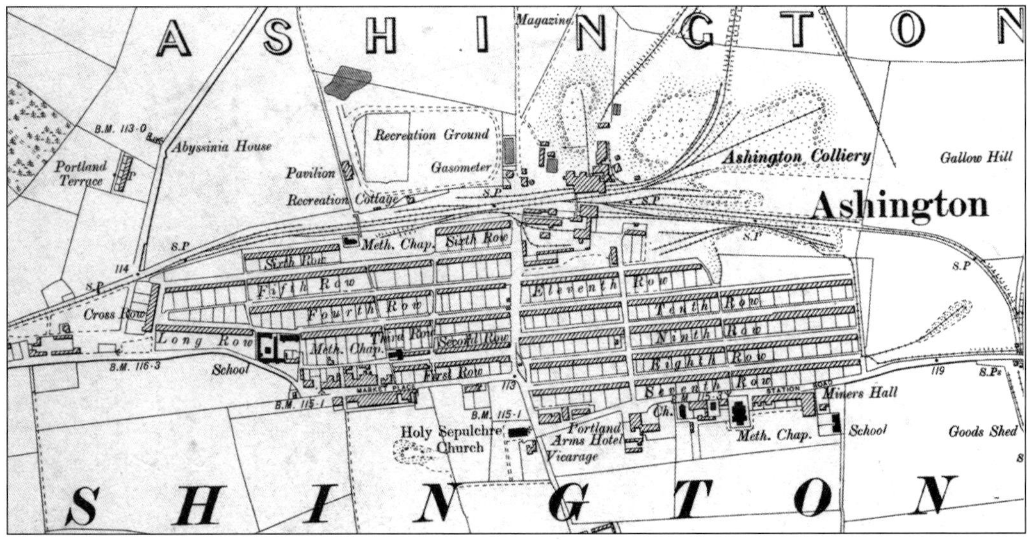

Ashington rows, OS map, 1898.

mounted messenger had arrived at Morpeth and as quickly as possible the Fire Brigade was called together. The fire engine set off at 11.15pm but was stopped at Whitefield (about half-way) and the men informed that their services were no longer required since the fire 'had been got under'.

On Sunday evening a public meeting was held in the Recreation Hall to find ways of helping families who had been affected by the fire.

They included a benefit performance by comedian Charles Coburn and his company and a public subscription. The buildings were covered by insurance but not the furniture and household property. The damage was estimated at £300 and nine families lost all their household possessions. They asked the colliery for a donation to the relief fund and the application was noted in the records of the Miners' Mutual Benefit Society but there is no mention of the outcome.

Miners were paid on a two-weekly basis and often went out on payday. Today we hope that the fire service will respond to a 999 call in minutes but in this case it took nearly two hours for the message about the fire to arrive in Morpeth (about four and a half miles) and another hour and a quarter to get the horse-drawn fire engine ready for service. It had covered only half the distance to the scene before the fire was extinguished.

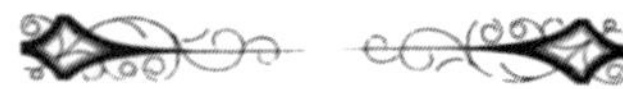

The Jarrow Boat / Disaster 26 Sept 1896 / 7 lives lost

above the inscription is engraved an empty rowing boat on water

reverse, a fern (62)

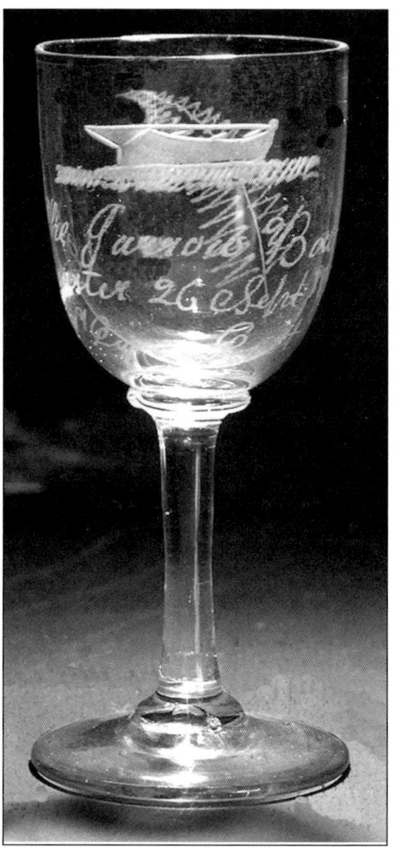

This incident was reported at some length in the *Newcastle Daily Journal* of September 28, 1896. In those days passengers between Jarrow on the south side of the river and Willington Quay and Howden on the north side were carried by two large ferries and a smaller steamer. The service did not run at night but one of the crew of the Tyne General Ferry Company picked up any passengers who missed the last ferry and took them across the river in a sculler boat. On the night in question eight tardy passengers were rowed across by boatman, Robert Young. The sea was calm that night and everything seemed normal at first. The two survivors said that about half-way across one of the women realised there was water around her feet. The boatman joked that they would have to swim before it rapidly became clear that the boat was filling with water and sinking. One passenger, John Osbome, who was 'well skilled in the art of natation' (a good swimmer) jumped overboard and swam for shore but the boat went down by the stern and the remaining occupants were left struggling in the water. Shouts and screams were heard on the shore and a rescue boat was launched. The second survivor, Thomas Campbell was found clinging to the half-submerged boat and taken ashore. The bodies of the two women were (like Ophelia) floating, buoyed up by their clothes and attempts were made over the next two hours to resuscitate them, but in vain. The September 30 edition of the paper, reporting the funeral of one of the women, mentioned that at that time none of the bodies of the five men had been recovered. The victims were James Bannister, Althea Bannister, his wife, Joseph Bell and his wife Sarah, Arthur Smee, Mr Waile and Robert Young. The Bannisters left eight children and the Bells five.

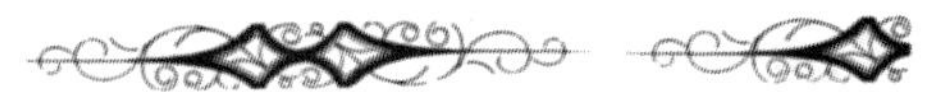

STRANGE BUT TRUE

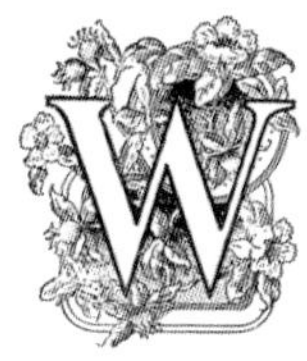e have found 44 glasses recording events of interest or notoriety that are peculiar to the North East. The first is intriguing because it pre-dates, by a long way, the period during which we believe these glasses were produced. However, the 50th anniversary of the event would place it firmly within our time scale.

Ten glasses relate to events of public interest or celebration. The remainder refer, in one way or another to individuals and of those, 16 inscriptions (47%) have a readily identifiable mining connection. When added to the 55 other specific mining records we have collected we suggest that this demonstrates the significant role of the mining community in promoting and encouraging a wider acceptance of this form of commemoration generally throughout the North East.

Another fact that seems to link these glasses very specifically to coalmining is the lack of any evidence connecting them to other major industries of the area. In spite of the long tradition of glassmaking in the North East and the fact that it became unionised and suffered strikes, it seems strange that we have not, so far, found a glass that refers to or commemorates glassmakers or glassmaking. This is equally true of shipbuilding; that other great industry of the Tyne and Wear. It would appear that the fashion for these glasses was firmly rooted in the mining community.

William Jobling Gibbetted at Jarrow Slake August 3rd 1832 (67)

This event had its origin in the bitter miners' strike of 1832 during which the pit owners imported lead miners in an effort to break the strike and evicted the coal miners from their tied cottages. On the afternoon of June 11, 1832, William Jobling and Ralph Armstrong were among a group of miners drinking at Turner's public house between South Shields and Jarrow. At about 5pm a local magistrate, Nicholas Fairless, was passing by on horseback when Jobling tried to beg some money from him. Fairless refused and Armstrong pulled him from his horse. In the resulting scuffle Fairless received injuries from which he died ten days later.

Armstrong escaped and was never arrested but Jobling was caught and tried at Durham assizes. Although he claimed that he had seen Armstrong strike the fatal blow, the jury

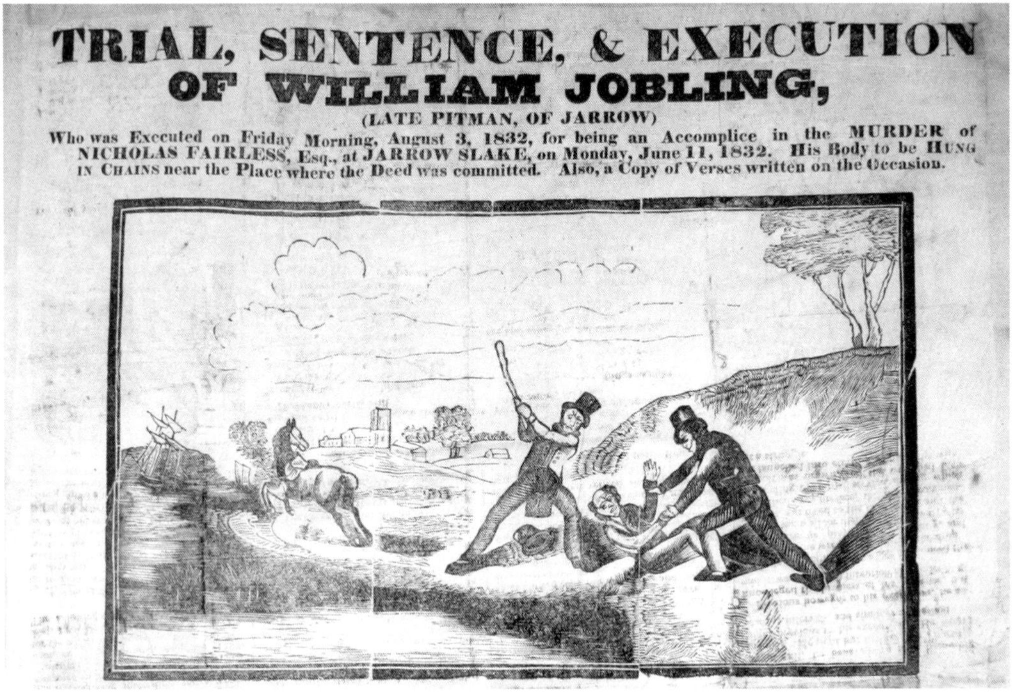

TRIAL, SENTENCE, & EXECUTION OF WILLIAM JOBLING,

(LATE PITMAN, OF JARROW)

Who was Executed on Friday Morning, August 3, 1832, for being an Accomplice in the **MURDER** of **NICHOLAS FAIRLESS**, Esq., at **JARROW SLAKE**, on Monday, June 11, 1832. His Body to be **HUNG IN CHAINS** near the Place where the Deed was committed. Also, a Copy of Verses written on the Occasion.

A newspaper covers the attack on Nicholas Fairless.

quickly found him guilty of murder and sentenced him to a public hanging. On August 3 Jobling was taken to the scaffold, which was guarded by 100 soldiers in case the miners tried to release him.

Gibbeting had been abolished in 1825 but a Bill was quickly pushed through Parliament for it to be reinstated for murder. On August 7 Jobling's body, covered in tar, re-clothed and put into an iron harness, was taken in a cart to the scene of the crime at Jarrow Slake and suspended from a 20 foot pole, 100 yards below the high water mark. Jobling's wife, Isabella, had a cottage near the Slake and would have been able to see her husband suspended there for the three weeks his body was displayed.

On August 31, after the guard had been removed, the body disappeared during the night. and it is thought that some of his friends came in by boat, cut him down and buried him at sea. Perhaps the mining connection was responsible for the production of this glass or it was possibly commissioned by one of Jobling's descendants.

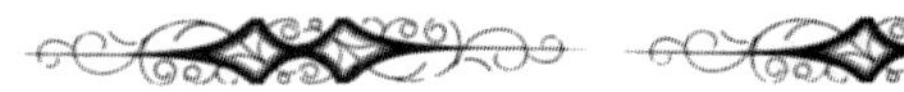

The following inscription relates to what was effectively a non-event.

Prize fight on Blyth Links / Between Stoke / of Seghill / and Mills of Gateshead / Stopped by Police 1849 (68)

On Monday November 5, 1849, a bare-knuckle fight scheduled to take place between two pitmen drew a huge crowd to Blyth links. Bets were invited for the large sums of £10 a side. Blyth had previously been the scene of a brutal fight between men called Gleghom and Riley, in which Riley was killed. The authorities were determined that such a thing should not happen again so the constables of Cowpen, Blyth and Newsham, with the help of the coast-guard officers and four police officers from North Shields, kept watch throughout the day and the fight was abandoned.

One has to speculate on why the glass was inscribed if the fight never took place and, once again, there is a discrepancy between the name quoted in the newspaper report (Stoker rather than Stoke) and the inscription on the glass.

Time Gun Milburn Place / Ballast Hill / North Shields / first Fired / 1863

reverse with a fern (70)

The hour of one o'clock was marked in North Shields by a gun, first a 6-pounder, replaced later by a 9-pounder, fired by hand. But on August 18, 1863, coinciding with a meeting of the British Association in Newcastle, a 32-pounder gun was installed on Ballast Hill and was fired daily at 1pm by an electrical current originating in the Edinburgh Observatory under the direction of Professor Piazzi Smyth. From around December 9, 1863, the 'direct current' to fire the gun came from Greenwich Observatory. On May 20, 1864, during a severe thunderstorm, the gun was accidentally fired by lightning and in 1865 it did not fire on November 5 and 6 'for want of electrical current' (*Shields Daily News* November 6, 1865). In 1869 it was silent 'for one or two

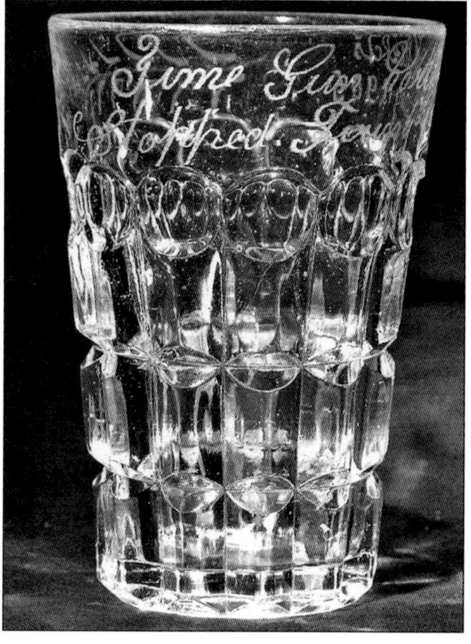

months' due to lack of funds but resumed firing when the funding issue was settled (*Shields Daily News*, March 16, 1889). The last firing was on August 31, 1905 and the gun was removed on September 9 the same year.

Ballast Hill was just that – a huge heap of waste material used as ballast, mainly by returning colliers, to replace the coal carried from Newcastle on their outward journeys.

Unfortunately, we no longer have a record of the type of glass on which the above inscription appeared but we have recently located a one pint pressed glass tumbler in Broadfield House Glass Museum that bears the inscription *Time Gun North Shields / Stopped Firing 13th Aug 1905* (111). It has always seemed unlikely to us that the first glass was contemporary with the 1863 date and now that we know of a glass marking the last firing, it seems more logical that glasses marking the duration of its operation were produced at the same time and at the later date.

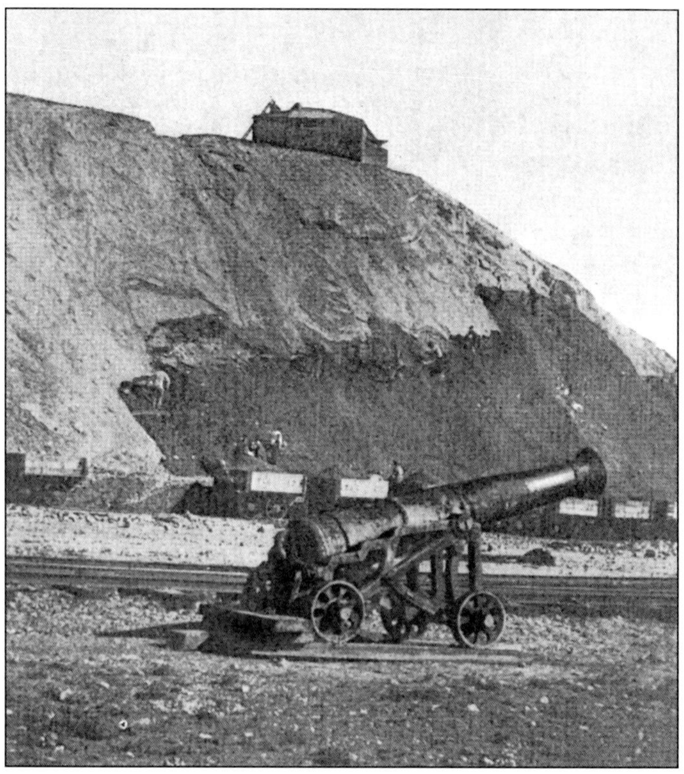

The Time Gun, post 1905, with Ballast Hill (being demolished) in the background.

Jesse Dawson Ewen / St Mary's Island / 1879

inscription enclosed within ferns. Reverse, a swan with leaves (71)

In 1855 George Ewen became a squatter on St Mary's Island, south of Seaton Sluice. There he built a cottage which was eventually turned into an Inn called The Freemason's Arms, also known locally as The Square and Compass. In 1894, Joseph Patterson, of Hartley East Farm,

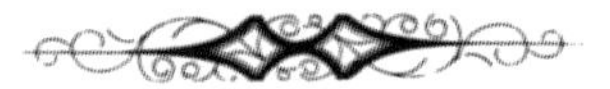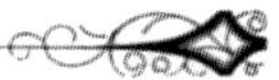

let a field on the mainland to the army for use as a rifle range. A dispute arose between him and Ewen about the right of way used by visitors to the inn and the danger of bullets flying over the island. Patterson accused Ewen and his friends of damaging his property and of opening the inn on a Sunday. In November 1895, Ewen was evicted because he was disputing the ownership of the house and his inn was taken over by John Harris Crisp with a covenant that it was to be used as a Temperance Hotel. The bailiffs took all of Ewen's possessions and furniture over the rocks to the headland and left them there.

The identity of the Ewen commemorated here is not clear. 'Jesse' was a most unusual first name for a man in 19th century England and it is likely that this was either a mis-spelling

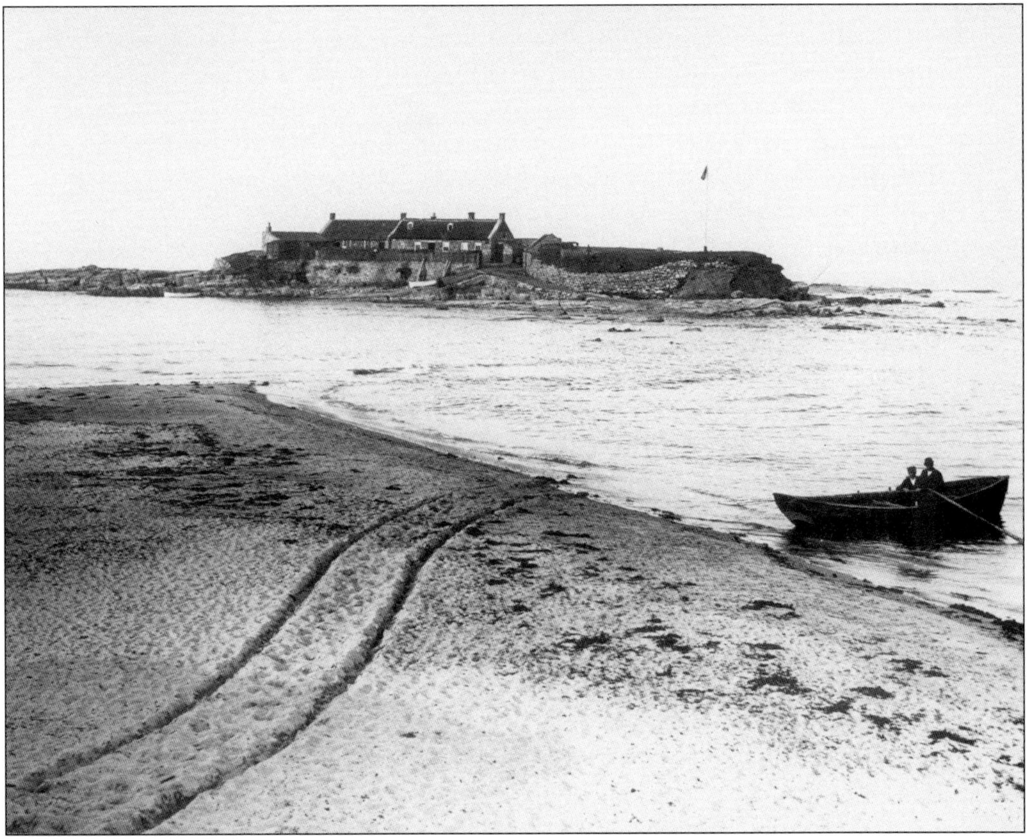

St Mary's Island, before the lighthouse was constructed, around 1890.

of Jessie or an idiosyncratic version of the girl's name. The Ewen family on St Mary's Island is well documented, but Jess(i)e Ewen does not appear in the records or on the 1891 census. Yet a male descendent of John Ewen had Dawson as a first name suggesting that the individual commemorated on the glass belonged to this family. No Jesse or Jessie Ewen was born, married or died in England or Wales in 1879 (St Catherine's House Index). However, the 1881 census lists a family of Ewens living in the west end of Newcastle upon Tyne at 53 Bell Street. They were James (27), George (23), Sarah (23), Mary (23), Francis 1 month and Jessie (3) (born in 1879). This group may have been two brothers with their wives and children. All are stated to have been born in Scotland. George Robertson Ewen, landlord of the pub on St Mary's Island, had also been born in Scotland. Perhaps the Newcastle Ewens were cousins and a commemorative glass bearing Jessie's year of birth was engraved for her on a visit to the island. This hypothesis may be challenged on two counts: we must assume that 'Jesse' is a mistake in the engraving but more important, the name 'Dawson' does not appear in the census. But to date we have no better suggestions.

This confusion highlights the difficulties that can be encountered when dealing with public records. Information supplied by the family may be incorrect or it may have been wrongly entered in the record. Details in newspaper reports are also sometimes at odds with either the public record or the inscription on the glass.

Succefs to Stobbs Wood [sic] / *New Church* / *The Good Shepherd* /*1895*

reverse *auld lang syne* cIover and tendrils (109)

Here is another example of a single-word place name being split into its syllables by an engraver, (such as Broom Hill, New Biggin and Cress Well). The small village of Stobswood in Northumberland, is about eight kilometres north of Ashington and adjacent to Widdrington Station. Stobswood Colliery opened in the 1880s and in 1896 was relatively small, employing 80 men and boys, 63 below, and 17 above ground.

Northumberland County Archives hold a manuscript book that lists the services held at the Chapel of the Good Shepherd at Stobswood Colliery, giving the name of the preacher and other details. This records services from June 3 to August 28, 1885. There is then a gap and the next entry is for September 1, 1895, suggesting that at this

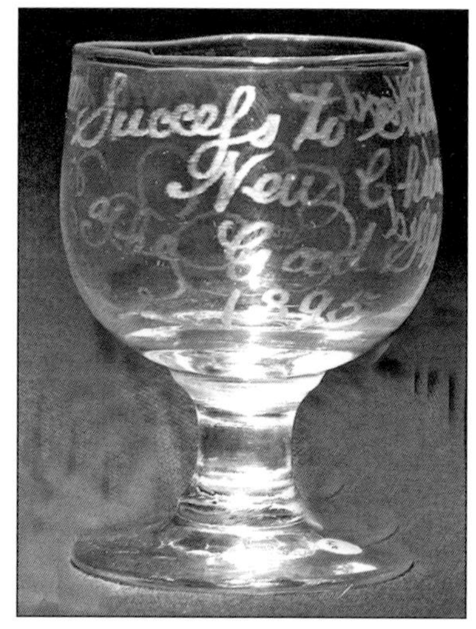

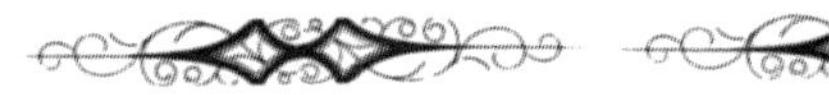

time the chapel may have re-opened and prompted the engraving of a glass. Unfortunately, careful search of both the *Morpeth Herald* and the *Blyth Weekly News* for several editions around this date fails to find any report of Stobswood Chapel.

Albert / Edward Dock opened 21 Aug 1884

reverse with a fern (74)

This event was attended by the Prince and Princess (Alexandra) of Wales, together with their two sons, Prince Albert Victor and Prince George (later King George V). The royal party stayed at Cragside at Rothbury as the guests of Lord Armstrong, travelling each day into Newcastle by special train.

After dinner and an overnight stay at Cragside they arrived in Newcastle at noon on August 20 where they opened Jesmond Dene as a public park. They lunched at St George's Hall, the drill hall of the Newcastle Volunteers, before opening the Natural History (Hancock) Museum and, finally, the reference department of the public library in New Bridge Street. They returned to Cragside for dinner. On August 21, back in Newcastle, they embarked on the steamer *Para-e-Amazonas*, a luxurious vessel chartered for the purpose, appropriately furnished and decorated, and sailed down the Tyne to Coble Dene. Here they found that the new dock was 'gaily decorated with flags and presented a gay appearance'.

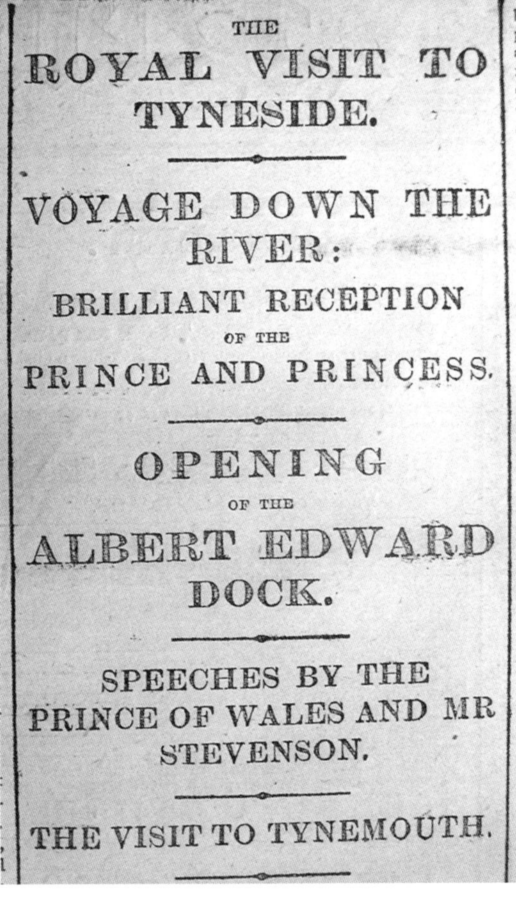

At 2.20pm the ship arrived at the main opening and slowly steaming into the dock broke

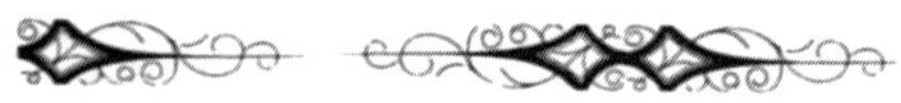

a ribbon stretched across the tidal entrance. The Prince named the dock Albert Edward Dock and declared it open. A banner was unfolded bearing the words 'The dock is declared open by HRH the Prince of Wales' and a royal salute was fired by a detachment of the Tynemouth Artillery Volunteers as the Royal steamer moved to her mooring place near to the luncheon pavilion. The dock is now the site of a factory outlet

POISSONS.
Saumon au Beurre Montpellier.
Filet de Soles à la Venitienne.
ENTREES ET VIANDS VARIEES.
Pâtés de Foie-Gras.   Cotelettes d'Agneau à la gelée.
Pigeons en Aspic.   Galantine de Volaillie.
Galantine de Veau.   Hûre de Sanglier.
Baron de Bœuf a la Garde du Roi.
Quartiers et Gigots d'Agneau.
Côtes et Aloyaux de Bœuf Garnis
Poulets Rôtis.   Poulardes à la Renaissance.
Jambons Garnis.   Langues Ecarlate.
Mayonnaise de Homard.
Salade à la Francaise.   Legumes Variées.
ENTREMETS.
Charlotte Russe.
Crême à la Fleur D'Orange.   Crême à la Vanille.
Gelée eu Maraschino.   Gelée au Vin.
Cômpote des Fruits.   Meringues.
DESSERT.

To give an idea of how public functions attended by Royalty were ordered in those days here is just part of the menu for lunch, as reported by Newcastle Daily Journal. The menu was printed on satin with hand-painted coats of arms.

centre, Royal Quays. The Royal party left for Edinburgh on August 22.

The Man Who Broke the Bank at Blyth (87)

The investigation into this glass revealed a major fraud that cost many people their savings.

By his own account, John Robinson started work at the age of 13 at a chemist's shop in Bottle Bank, Gateshead but left after a few months to be apprenticed to a draper in South Shields. He had also at some point served on one or two sailing ship voyages, stowing sails. After four years in South Shields he moved to Blyth and, aged 18, joined the local temperance movement. Under his eventual leadership the movement recruited 700 members in Blyth. Robinson later became a Wesleyan and afterwards joined the Congregational Church of Blyth, raising funds for their chapel and occasionally taking services and preaching. He was also familiar at Salvation Army meetings.

Over the years he established himself as a leading figure in Blyth, 'identifying himself with all kinds of commercial ventures, religious and temperance and social movements, whilst he also at one time held most of the public appointments in the town'. He was clerk of the

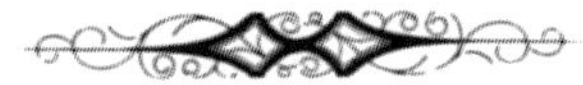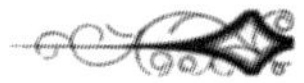

Cowpen Local Board, secretary of the Northumbrian Building Society, had been clerk of the South Blyth Local Board for ten years, clerk of the Cowpen Burial Board, secretary to the Blyth and Cowpen Gas Company, secretary to the Shipwrecked Fishermen and Mariners' Society and was associated with the printing works of Robinson Bros., who published the newspaper the *Blyth Examiner* as well as *Robinson's Almanac*. He also ran a stationer's shop, was a sub-postmaster and owned the Central Hall in Blyth, purchased for £3100. Finally he was secretary and manager of the Blyth Deposit and Advance Bank. He lived in Monkseaton.

In mid-February 1894, rumours spread that Mr Robinson was bankrupt. Cheques drawn to pay tradesmen and workers employed by the South Blyth Board and the Blyth and Cowpen Gas Company were unaccounted for and the accounts of the Burial Board showed a deficiency. Mr Robinson was not available but his son claimed that his father was ill in London and asked for any action to be postponed. Unconvinced, the Board took out a warrant to arrest Robinson. The position of the Blyth Deposit and Advance Bank generated the most anxiety. Formed six years previously, very little was known about its assets or securities. John Robinson was the proprietor, secretary, treasurer and auditor; indeed the only official.

John Robinson had last been seen in Blyth on February 13. By February 24, depositors, 'entertaining the gravest fears that they will lose their hard earned savings', found the doors of the bank closed and nobody available to answer questions. Some people wept in the street. All bank books, letters and other documents had disappeared from the office of the bank. 'It is one of the most gigantic and ramified commercial collapses which has ever figured in the commercial life of Blyth'. Mr Robinson, 'a little over sixty years', was reported in the *Newcastle Daily Journal* of

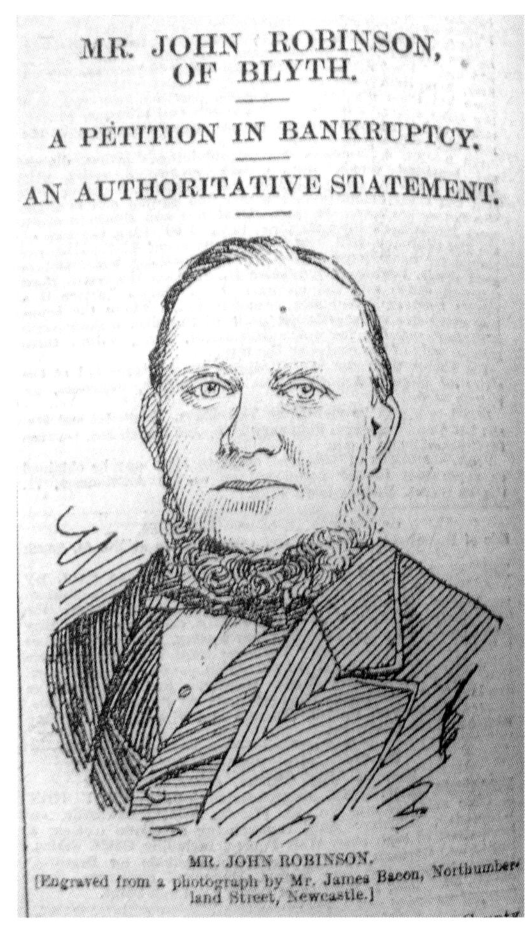

MR. JOHN ROBINSON.
[Engraved from a photograph by Mr. James Bacon, Northumberland Street, Newcastle.]

February 24 to be in Paris but this information was 'totally discredited' in Blyth, according to the *Blyth Weekly News* of March 3. However, the March 24 edition of the same paper reported that 'It is now understood definitely that Mr John Robinson, of Blyth, is in France, desirous of presenting himself at Newcastle for examination.' On April 21, with John Robinson still missing, the leading article of the *Blyth Weekly News* described the affair as 'one of the most colossal financial collapses which has ever blackened the records of local and commercial life … All Mr Robinson's trumpetings … about it being a sound financial concern … have come to naught, and were loudest when the bank was rottenest.' The official statement of the bankruptcy showed a deficiency of £10,240 7s 9d. A final meeting of the creditors was held on April 24. Deaths of various John Robinsons were reported from around the world but John Robinson of Blyth, the subject of the glass, was never seen again. He left a wife and two young children.

Seaton Sluice / Bridge Opened 2 May /1894

reverse clover (90)

The dedication and opening of public works was conducted with considerable pomp and ceremony during the 19th century and this relatively minor occasion was no exception. The formal ceremony of demolishing the Briar Dene Toll-gate at Whitley to open a direct free road from Tynemouth to Blyth and the opening of the Seaton Sluice Bridge were reported in the the *Morpeth Herald and Reporter* of May 5 1894. The *Blyth Weekly News* of the same date printed a shortened version of the report.

The ceremony was performed by the Rt. Hon. Sir Matthew W. Ridley, Bart, MF, chairman of the Northumberland Council after he

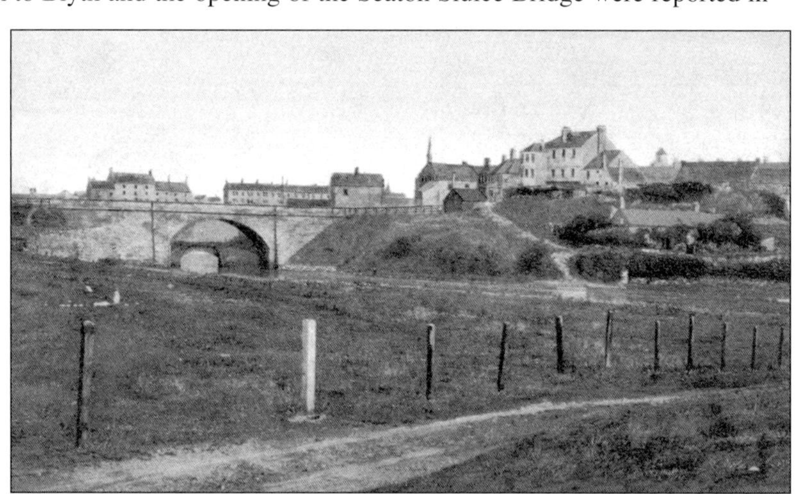

Seaton Sluice Bridge.

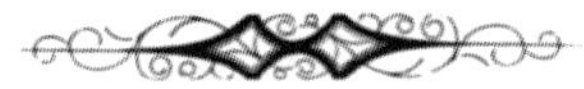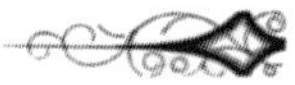

and other dignitaries, such as the Mayor of Tynemouth, enjoyed lunch at the Whitley Club. The party left the club in carriages and drove to Briar Dene toll-bar in torrential rain. Despite the weather, a large number of people were there to cheer Sir Matthew when he declared the road free for ever to traffic. Sir Matthew 'then knocked down the obnoxious barrier [we are not told how exactly] amid the plaudits of those assembled'. Returning to their carriages the official party drove to Seaton Sluice. It was still pouring but a large crowd waited to watch Sir Matthew declare the bridge open. The ceremony was repeated on the other side of the bridge. After 13 more speeches, addresses and presentations a dinner was held in the village school to celebrate the event. Presumably, by this time, Sir Matthew was back at Blagdon Hall with his feet up.

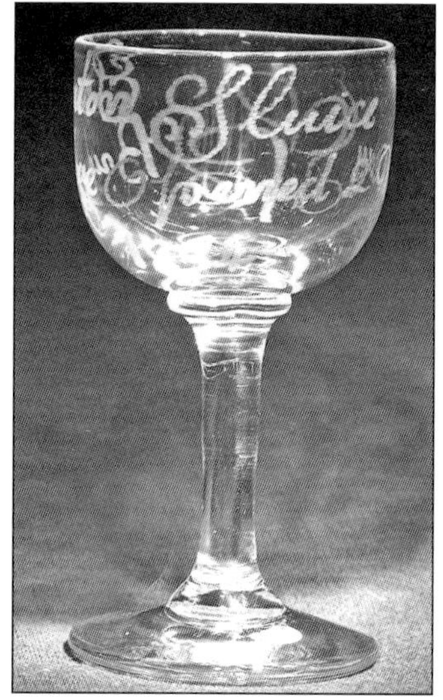

Holywell / Bridge / Opened 20 June 1894

reverse fern (93)

There has been a village of Holywell, on the southern approach to Seaton Delaval in Northumberland since 1161. According to the *Newcastle Daily Chronicle* in 1873 'Holywell village is not by any means a clean place; there seems a want of drainage and a deficiency of sanitary arrangements', but it is more attractive now. The well was dedicated to St Mary, one of several chemical or healing springs in the dene of Seaton Burn. It was situated in private land known as The Park near to the Holywell Bridge. This spring apparently tasted of ink and iron and it was said that the water rose in 'predictable bubbles'. To-day only a few stones of the original well remain.

Holywell Bridge carries the A192 road across Seaton Burn immediately south of the village about 2.5 kilometres west and upstream of the larger Seaton Sluice bridge that had opened a few weeks earlier. The bridge at Holywell is best viewed to-day from the old, stone bridge, now carrying a bridleway and crossing the Burn a few yards upstream. The new version was never a handsome structure; a single span of iron girders lies across stone abutments and these are now kept vertical by massive wooden, graffiti-covered buttressing. After crossing south over the old bridge, a path leads under the new bridge and along the attractive Burn to the Well and beyond.

The Alnmouth Riot / 22 Sept 1895 / Better Luck to the Police / & / The Rev Mr Brailford's [sic] /recovery

reverse with a yacht between vertical ferns (103)

The yacht is virtually the same as that engraved on the reverse of the Four Blyth Men glass (61); the stays forward of the mast and the pennant from the masthead are identical.

This incident is reported in the *Newcastle Daily Journal,* the *Newcastle Daily Chronicle,* the *Morpeth Herald* and the *Alnwick and County Gazette*. At the annual 'feast' at Alnmouth on September 22, a number of pitmen arrived by boat (possibly stolen) from Amble, five miles south along the coast, and became noisy and quarrelsome. The local policeman, PC Richardson, was called to the Schooner Hotel at about 8pm to eject them. He was assaulted by two men one of whom, named Linen, hit him in the eye, knocking him down and taking his truncheon. The constable followed Linen and arrested him. Linen was taken to Amble by a sergeant and constable who had been summoned from Alnwick by telephone. Meanwhile the rest of the gang attempted to escape by sailing back to Amble but were frustrated by lack of wind and returned to Alnmouth 'infused with a spirit of revenge as well as frenzied by drink'. PC Richardson's house was besieged and his windows smashed as the 'rough men' went around the village, assaulting people and breaking windows. The Rev. Edmund J. Brailsford, Wesleyan Chairman of the District, was on holiday at Alnmouth, staying at the house of a friend. He had preached that evening at the Chapel, returned to the house and was

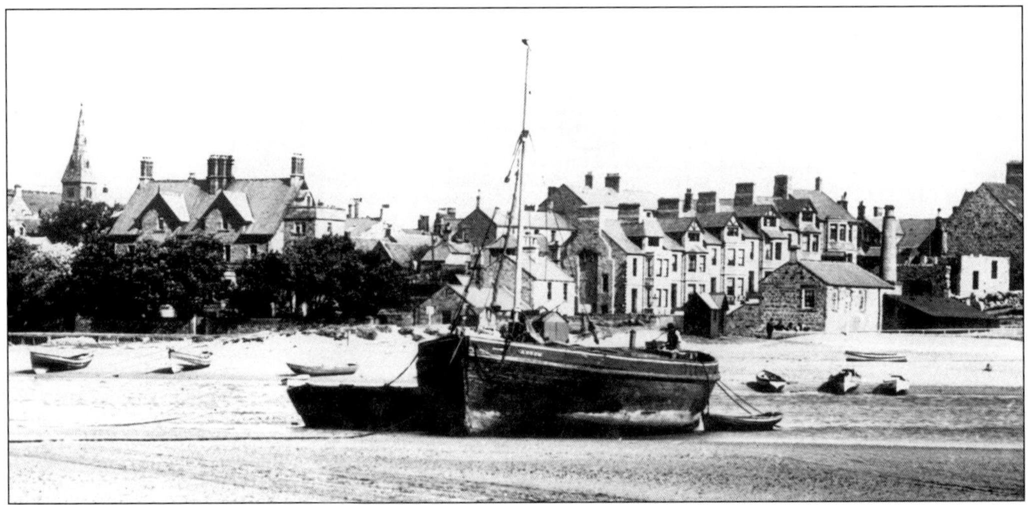

Alnmouth in the 1890s.

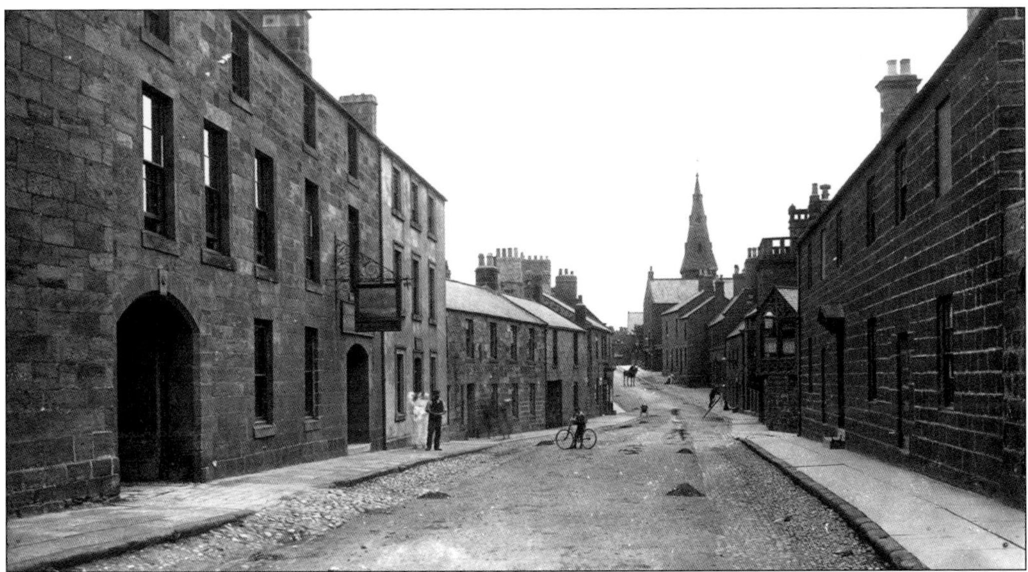

The Schooner Hotel, left, in the early 1900s.

sitting in an upstairs room when a stone came through the window. He and his son went downstairs to investigate, confronted some men which provoked a violent response. Rev. Brailsford was hit on the face with a stone with such force that he fractured his cheekbone. His assailant continued hitting him while he lay on the ground. His son was also attacked.

A Dr Ridley, who happened to be staying in Alnmouth pronounced the Rev. Brailsford's injuries as serious but not dangerous. The whole village, inhabitants and visitors, was now aroused; some of them, armed with sticks, surrounded a number of the rioters although four forded the river and escaped towards Amble. More police had arrived, a sergeant and two PCs from Alnwick and two sergeants and two PCs from Amble, and nine men were arrested. Remanded in custody, they appeared at Alnwick Magistrates Court and William Linen of Amble was sentenced to six months imprisonment with hard labour. The remaining eight men were later charged with 'unlawfully, riotously and tumultuously assembling together to the disturbance of the public and feloniously and with force doing injury and damage to certain houses in the village of Alnmouth'. After the Rev. Brailsford had given evidence the men were committed for trial at the Quarter Sessions.

A slightly different version of the riot is given by Ella Dodds in her *Memories of Alnmouth*. She states that the Percy Volunteers, who had headquarters at Alnwick and detachments in various villages, competed in an artillery firing contest, firing out to sea at Alnmouth on the day in question. The competition was won by Alnmouth much to the chagrin of Amble, and it was this that sparked the riot. However, although the annual feast would seem an appropriate time to hold this event, none of the newspaper accounts mention any artillery competition. Isabel Wright (*Alnmouth Ancient and Modern*) states that the gun used by the Percy Artillery Corps at Alnmouth was dismantled in 1893. Moreover, Ella Dodds' assertion that there was no resident policeman in Alnmouth at the time is clearly incorrect. Ms. Wright gives a short account of the riot and concludes: 'It is interesting to know that some commemorative glasses were made and at least one still exists.' She cites a virtually identical engraving to the one above.

In Memory of John RC Findlater / Died Feb 22nd 1890 / Aged 13^{1}/$_{2}$ Years

(79)

This inscription is unusual for two reasons. First because it relates to a young man who lived in Philip Street in the middle of Newcastle upon Tyne and had no obvious connection with the mining industry since his father was a railway guard. He died of tuberculosis and is not recorded as having any occupation so he was either still at school or was too weakly to have a job. Since he is unlikely to have established any reputation for himself within the community one is drawn to the conclusion that this glass was made as a memento to mark his funeral. Secondly, he is remembered on a large glass jug which is elaborately engraved to a much higher standard than was usual. The only other instance of such a jug is that for Lady Grey in Beamish Museum. Since the family lived in Newcastle one may also speculate on where the jug was engraved. Was it executed in the city, in response to a widespread local tradition, by an engraver who was more proficient than those working on the great majority of glasses we have recorded?

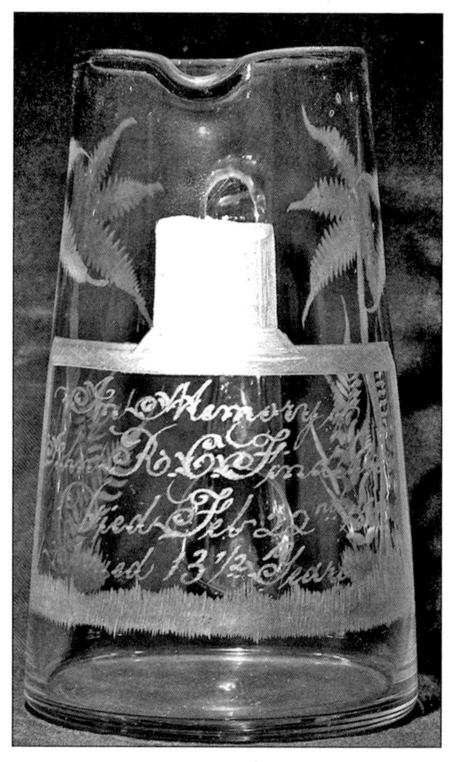

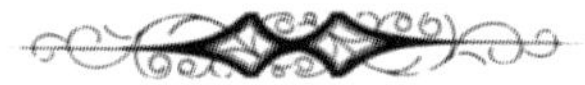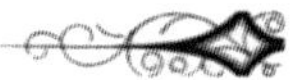

Andrew Colvin / Who Died at Blyth / 26 April 1895 Aged 84 Years.

reverse *Rock of Ages cleft for Me* (100)

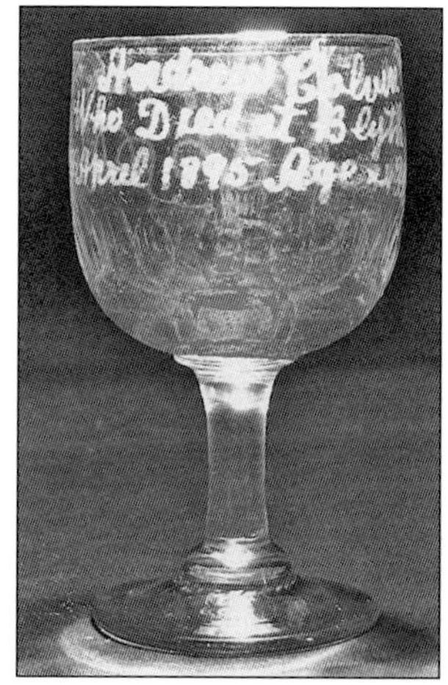

Andrew Colvin was a well-known character in 19th century Blyth. He was born on September 11, 1811, in a cottage near Blyth lent to Methodists. At the age of nine he went down the pit at Cowpen Colliery, working 15 hours a day as a trapper for ten pence a day. A trapper opened and closed wooden ventilation doors to allow traffic to pass; it was a job for young boys starting out on their mining careers. At this point Colvin had received little education, being taught first by a miner then at a dame school. He later became a putter and finally, for 50 years, a hewer. Although offered an easier job, he refused since the shifts underground allowed him more freedom to work for the Methodists.

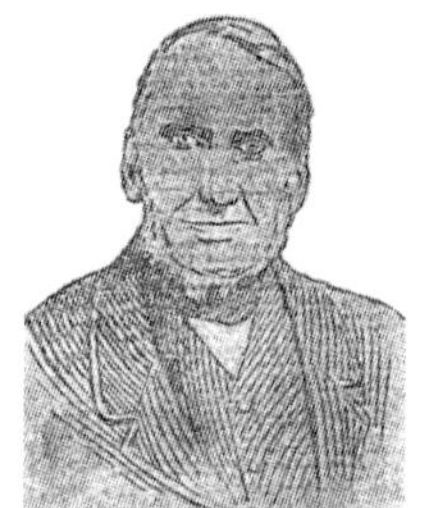

In 1834 he conducted the first Wesleyan service in Newbiggin and by 1841 he was preaching locally in Blyth. He was married in 1838 to Isabella Kilgour, a devout Christian and temperance worker who bore him four sons and three daughters. At the age of 32 he passed a trial sermon and theological examination and was received as a fully accredited Wesleyan preacher at Monkseaton. His reputation extended throughout Northumberland, Durham and especially Hexham and in Blyth he became known as 'St Andrew'. He was a major attraction there on a Saturday evening preaching from his mobile pulpit in the Market Place. He was buried at Cowpen Cemetery.

Succefs to Charles / Fenwick MP / 1895

reverse *Hee's* [sic] *a Jolly / good fellow* and clover leaf (105)

Charles Fenwick was born in Cramlington in 1850 and, after attending a colliery school, started work at Bebside pithead at the age of nine. A year later he went underground. Although active in the Northumberland Miners' Association and a delegate to the Trade Union Congress in 1884, he continued to work in the pit until 1885. In this year he was elected the Liberal Member of Parliament for the newly created Wansbeck division. He successfully contested the seat in 1886, 1892, 1895, 1900, 1906 and 1910. He regularly attended the Durham Miners' Gala between 1886 and 1909.

Fenwick served on several Royal Commissions and continued to be an active member of the Northumberland Miners' Association. In the 1910 Coronation Honours List he was made a Privy Councillor and in December 1917 he was given a complimentary luncheon by the Northumberland Miners to celebrate his 32 consecutive years in Parliament. He was also a Primitive Methodist Church preacher.

He fell ill and complications set in about ten days before his death on April 20, 1918. He was buried in St Andrew's Cemetery, Newcastle. Among the many mourners were representatives of the Miners' Federation, the Northumberland Miners' Association, the Durham Miners' Association, the Northumberland Coal Owners' Association, The Northern Counties Permanent Building Society, the Lord Mayor, and the deputy Lord Mayor of Newcastle.

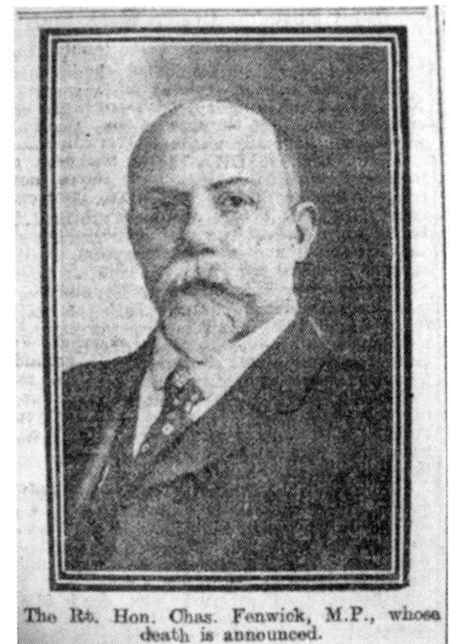

The Rt. Hon. Chas. Fenwick, M.P., whose death is announced.

In Honour Of / Lord Walkworth (sic) */ Wishing him Succefs / In the future /*
1895 (97)

The seventh duke and duchess of Northumberland had 13 children, of whom six died prematurely. Their eldest son, Henry Algernon, was known as Lord Warkworth until 1899, when he was granted the title Lord Percy. Warkworth Castle came into the hands of the Percys in 1332. For centuries the castle was the favourite residence of the Percys when in Northumberland but the first Duke decided to develop Alnwick as his northern seat and Warkworth fell into disrepair.

Henry Percy was a man of outstanding intellect who seemed certain to attain high political office. Educated at Eton and Christ Church College, Oxford, in 1895 he was elected Conservative MP for South Kensington and retained his seat until his death. From 1902 he was Under Secretary of State

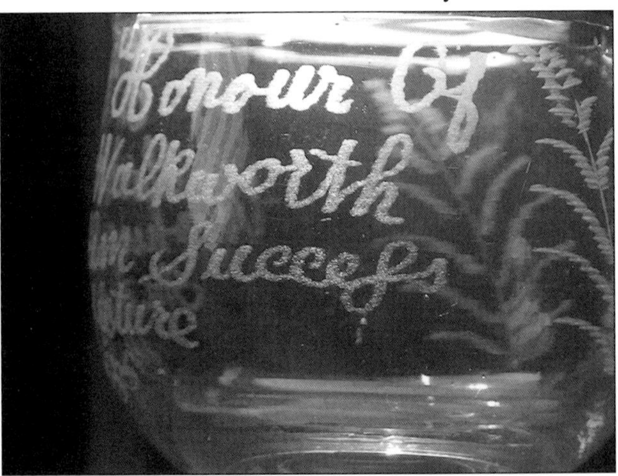

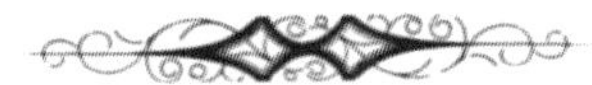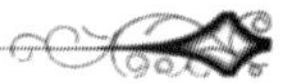

for India and the Under Secretary of State for Foreign Affairs. In the general election of January 1906, the Liberals won a landslide victory. Percy retained his seat but he never again held office. At the end of 1909 he died of pneumonia in the Gare du Nord Hotel, Paris.

This glass, and the glass commemorating the re-election of Charles Fenwick at the same general election must surely have been engraved by the same hand. Both spell 'success' as 'succefs' and both contain mistakes of spelling ('Hees' and 'Walkworth').

In Memory Of / Robert Lancelot Booth / Died 25 Nov 1891 / Ashington Colliery

reverse *gone but not forgotten* and a fern (84)

Robert Booth was the eldest son of one of the owners of Norwood Collieries, near Bishop Auckland. His death, 'under painfully sudden circumstances' was reported at some length in the *The Morpeth Herald* of November 28, 1891. At suppertime Booth left the table before eating anything and headed for the bathroom. His wife heard a noise and found her husband in an 'apoplexy fit'. He died the next morning. As manager of Ashington Colliery he had a reputation for looking after the miners and supporting them in their efforts for social and intellectual improvement.

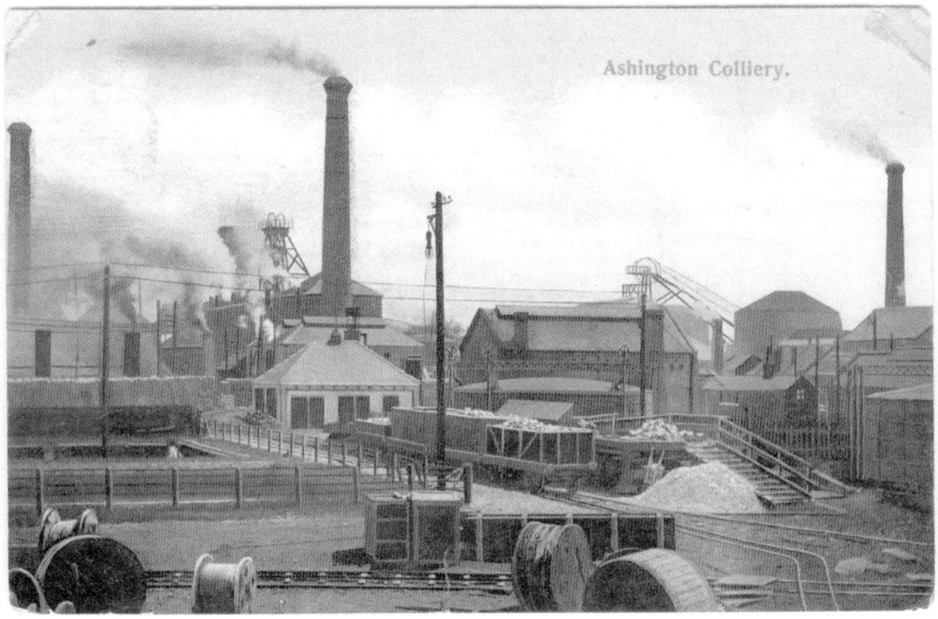

Another notable mine official was remembered with the following inscription:

In Memory of / Thomas Henry M Stratton / Who Died 29 May 1894 / Cramlington House / Age 42 years.

reverse *In the Sweet / by and by* and a clover leaf (92)

After working in Monmouthshire, he was appointed manager of the Cramlington Coal Company's pits in 1877. He was chairman of the Cramlington School Board, vice-chairman of the Cramlington Local Board and a member of the Joint Committee of the Northumberland Coal Owners' Association. He was remembered for his bravery during the rescue attempt after the explosion at Seaham on September 8, 1880. He died from pneumonia brought on by a chill. 'In the sweet by and by' is a quotation from a hymn by Ira David Sankey (1840-1908): 'In the sweet by and by We shall meet on that beautiful shore'.

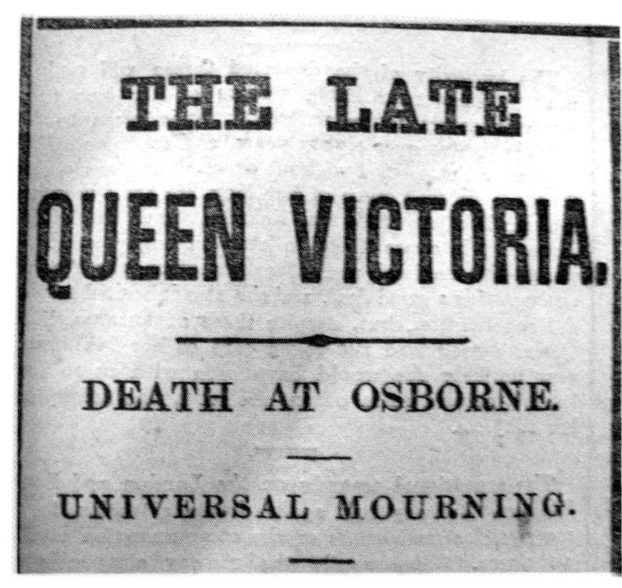

THE WIDER WORLD

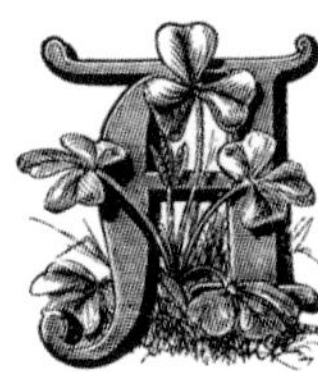fter 1895 the custom of commemorating deaths or local events on glass appears to have declined sharply. We have one record for 1899, Isabella Vasey (110). Mining disasters, and local boating accidents, however, did continue to be commemorated up to the end of World War I. This section lists some of the glasses that conform to the pattern and style of all those we have already discussed but record events that occurred outside North East England. For the first time they appear to reflect North Eastern reaction to the general mood of patriotism during war-time or to catastrophic events that aroused the concern and sympathy of the whole country. There appears to be no clear reason for this change unless the fashion for remembering local events had run its course and the engravers were forced to turn their attention to events of more general significance in an effort to stay in business. At all events, even the demand for mining commemoratives seems to have expired by the end of World War I and the market for engraved glass that had commemorated so many aspects of life in the North East came to an end. The isolated example of the Hindmarsh glass (112) in 1934 suggests that whoever commissioned it had some memory of the popular fashion of 40 years earlier but we do not think it represents an ongoing tradition.

The War England Always Ready (114)

Although it is conceivable that this citation is unique, referring to the Ashanti War (1874), the Kaffir War or Second Afghan War (1878), the Zulu War (1879) or the First Boer War (1881), it is much more likely that it was engraved in 1899 or 1914 to commemorate the start of either the Second Boer (Transvaal) War or that of World War I. There were a number of glasses engraved in 1899 that commemorated the start of the conflict, General Buller at the front and the siege of Ladysmith (see below), but we know of only one commemorating the start of World War I. This includes capital lettering, common at the time, and therefore 1899 seems the most likely.

Transvaal War / Commenced 11 Oct / 1899 (115)

Until 1886, when gold was discovered in the Witwatersrand, an uneasy balance existed between the Dutch-descended Afrikaners or Boers and the British settlers in South Africa. The British were mostly in Cape Province and Natal whereas the Boers dominated the Transvaal or South African Republic and the Orange River colony, living in close-knit, isolated communities. It was the opening up of the Rand that upset the balance. The lure of gold brought an influx of British and other nationalities into the Transvaal. The Boers, who controlled the political process of the province, treated them as 'Uitlanders' (literally 'outlanders'), refusing them voting and other rights and tension gradually built up. After years of hostility the British decided to increase their 12,000-strong army contingent in South Africa to a force that eventually numbered 500,000. This finally prompted an ultimatum, probably drafted by Jan Smuts, one of the guerrilla leaders, and issued by President Kruger of the Transvaal, demanding withdrawal of British troops from the Transvaal border, removal of all troops who had arrived since June 1 and return of all troops then on the high seas bound for South Africa. Unless 'an immediate and affirmative answer' to these demands was received by 5pm on Wednesday, October 11, 1899, the Transvaal would consider the British to have declared war.

Transvaal War / Three Cheers / for General White / at Ladysmith / 1899 (116)

British forces under the command of Lt. General Sir George White VC suffered more than 1,200 casualties on 'Mournful Monday', October 30, 1899. They were driven back to

Ladysmith where they were besieged from November 2, 1899, until relieved by General Buller on February 28 1900. Sir George White was sent back to England and sacked for this incompetence. Under those circumstances 'Three Cheers' has an ironic ring to it! General Buller is noted on other glasses (117,118).

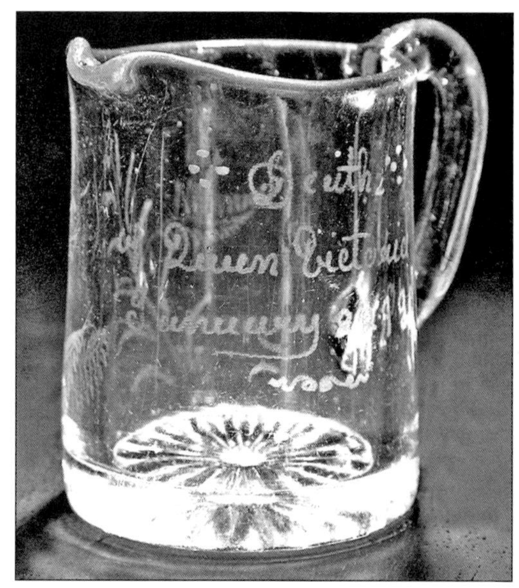

Death / of Queen Victoria / January 22 1901 (120)

This inscription appears on a small pressed glass jug and is unusual in being the only reference to Queen Victoria on any of the glasses we have seen.

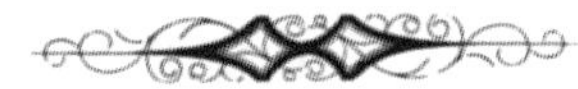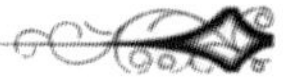

King Edward VII / Crowned 20 June / 1902
(122)

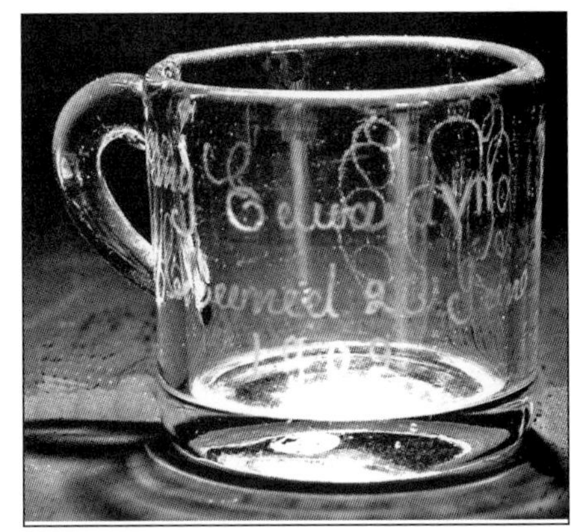

This inscription, on a small tankard, must have been engraved at some time before the Coronation since the King fell ill just before June 20 and became one of the first people in England to be operated on for appendicitis. The Coronation finally took place on August 9. One can assume that this glass was produced for ordinary retail sale in competition with the range of other souvenirs that were being produced by the pressed glass companies. A similar event occurred in 1936 when huge quantities of souvenirs were made obsolete by the abdication of Edward VIII.

Coronation / of King George / June 22 1911 / Coronation of Queen Mary / June 22 1911

reverse with crossed flags

This inscription appears on a jug, but pairs of glasses with separate inscriptions for the King and Queen have been recorded (see 124 & 125).

WHITE STAR LINE / TITANIC SINKING
(127)

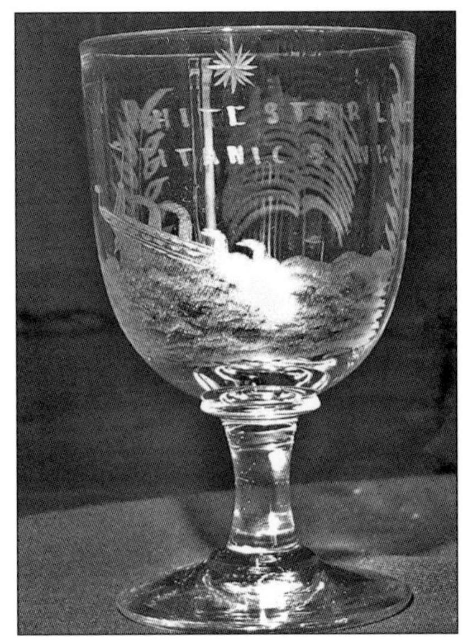

The 'E' of 'WHITE' lacks the central horizontal stroke and above it there is an engraved star. Below is an engraved ship half submerged in a rough sea with smoke coming from all four funnels.

The engraving on this glass is highly fanciful since the ship sank in a dead calm sea and the after funnel was a dummy. It is also unusual for being undated. The date was April 15, 1912 when the ship, carrying 2,224 passengers and crew, sank on her maiden voyage after hitting an iceberg south of Newfoundland. There were only 711 survivors.

A virtually identical specimen is in the Broadfield

House Glass Museum which does have the central horizontal stroke to the 'E' but it is very thin and faint. Broadfield House also has a blown glass tumbler inscribed in capital letters: *TITANIC SUNK APRIL 15 1912 1615 LIVES LOST*. The official loss of life was 1513, suggesting that this is an example of a glass being engraved soon after the disaster and before the true number was established.

Empress of Ireland Disaster May 29 1914 (129)

This was a major disaster that must have been reported in newspapers, both national and provincial, throughout the world. The *Newcastle Daily Journal* devoted four columns to a report of the 'Terrible Disaster'. The SS *Empress of Ireland* was built in Glasgow in 1906. She was the sister ship of the SS *Empress of Britain* and they were the two largest ships in the Canadian Pacific fleet. At the time of the disaster she was carrying 787 passengers (1st Class: 77, 2nd Class: 206, 3rd Class: 504) and a crew of more than 400, under the command of Commander H.J. Kendall. Bound from Quebec to Liverpool, at 2am on Friday, May 29, 1914 she was off Father Point at the mouth of the St Lawrence River. In dense fog she was rammed amidships by the Tyne-built Norwegian collier *Storstad*, bound for Quebec, creating a huge hole in her side into which a 'deluge of water instantly poured'. She sank in 20 minutes.

339 people were saved by the mail tender *Lady Evelyn* and a further 60 by the pilot boat *Eureka* but the speed with which the vessel sank, and the time of the collision, inevitably led to great loss of life, totalling perhaps 800.

Commander Kendall's other claim to fame is that in 1910, when in command of the SS *Montrose*, he identified one of his passengers 'Mr Robinson' as the murderer Dr H.H. Crippen. The description of the wanted man stated that Crippen had false teeth, so to check his theory Kendall told his suspect a joke. 'Robinson' laughed and revealed teeth that were loose and obviously false, so Kendall contacted Scotland Yard by radio-telegraphy (the first time that radio had been used for police purposes). Crippen was arrested.

THE LUSITANIA / SUNK / MAY 7 1915

reverse with crossed Union flags (130)

This glass recalls a tragedy that was closely associated with the entry of the USA into World War I. The RMS *Lusitania* (32,000 tons) was the largest, fastest and one of the most luxurious passenger liners on the trans-Atlantic run and was the flagship of the Cunard fleet. Docked in New York after her maiden voyage in 1907, she was dubbed 'a skyscraper adrift'. When she left New York on her final voyage, most of her passengers were content to ignore German

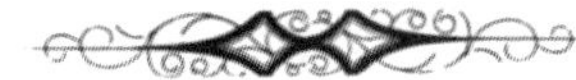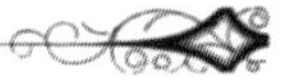

warnings of unrestricted submarine warfare. The Americans had been advised against taking passage on British vessels in a notice in American morning newspapers on the day that the ship sailed, May 1, but her master, Captain Turner, did not enforce lifebelt and lifeboat drills fearing passenger alarm and resistance.

She was torpedoed without warning by the German submarine, *U20* at 2.10pm on May 7 off the southern coast of Ireland. She quickly developed a steep list to starboard with a result that most of the port lifeboats could not be launched and many of the starboard boats swung out too far to be boarded. She sank within 18 minutes. Of the 1,257 passengers and 702 members of the crew, 785 passengers, (including 128 Americans), perished together with 413 members of the crew, a total loss of life of 1,198. The German assertion that the ship was carrying arms for the Allies was denied by Great Britain and the USA, but in fact she was carrying a small amount of ammunition that, in theory, made her a legitimate target. The Germans claimed that the ammunition had exploded, contributing to the disaster, but recent marine archaeology suggests that it was coal dust in the near-empty bunkers triggered by the single torpedo that blew a cavernous hole in her side.

Although America did not declare war on Germany until 1917 'Remember the Lusitania' was a popular slogan and it is accepted that the sinking was a significant factor in the ending of US neutrality.

The crossed Union flags on the reverse are identical to those on the glasses commemorating the start of World War I (128) and the death of Lord Kitchener (1916) (131). All three glasses are engraved in capital letters.

THE WAR WITH / England & Germany / aug 4 1914

(128)

This inscription is interesting in that it the only example we have seen combining upper case letters with cursive script. Why the change to capital letters took place is not clear but it may be that it was easier and therefore quicker and cheaper to engrave in this manner.

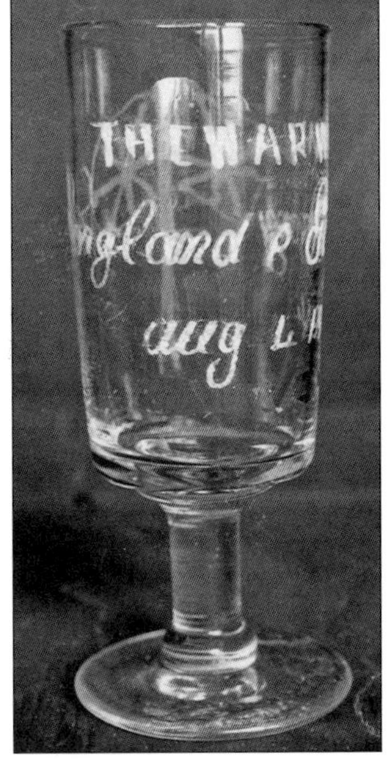

THROUGH A GLASS DARKLY

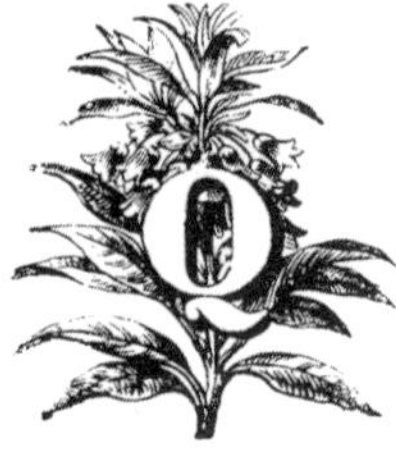

uestions still remain as to why and for whom the commemorative glasses of the North East were made, and who made and inscribed them.

It is obvious that we are dealing with a much larger group of glasses than realised up to now. While the mining glasses were seen as an isolated group it was generally supposed that they were produced for sale in order to raise funds for the dependents of those who were either killed or injured in accidents. (C. Hajdamach, *English Glass 1800-1914* p.173, and J.H. Wilson, *Glass Making on Wearside*, p.24) but we have yet to find documentary evidence to support this view. If we accept this premise with regard to major disasters that were reported in the national press, were these modest glasses also sold country wide? Again, we have found no evidence.

It is intriguing that among the glasses that survive, in addition to those recording multiple deaths, some are inscribed for individual miners whose demise would have been reported only locally, while others commemorate non-fatal incidents. We shall never know how many of these accidents were recorded in this way but, given the frequency of accidents in coal mines, we might expect to have found more of them recorded on glass than those we have so far identified. If only a proportion of the accidents that took place were recorded, who decided which ones or which individuals should be commemorated?

The glasses which turn up most frequently today are those for the Hartley Colliery disaster in 1862 and the Victoria Hall disaster in 1883 so it may be safely assumed that they were produced in considerable quantities. If they were sold for fund raising purposes, who commissioned them to be engraved, how were they sold and who collected the money and distributed the proceeds?

The reaction to both of these disasters was the establishment of relief funds on a national scale, promoted and administered by the local authority. The final report into the Hartley Disaster, for example, reported that the relief fund grew to over £83,000 during its existence and, in addition to the administration of relief locally, made two large grants to other miners' organisations as well as several smaller grants to other mining disaster funds. By 1901 only four or five Hartley widows were still alive to draw a pension and the fund, still wealthy, was finally wound up in 1909. Given the size of the fund it is difficult to see what difference the modest proceeds from a few cheap drinking glasses would have made unless they could be seen in the context of an immediate and local response in the early days following the tragedy and before the relief fund was fully established.

If a general practice had developed of producing and selling glasses to provide relief funds for the less dramatic accidents the local Miners' Union lodge would seem a logical choice to take on the responsibility. We have not seen the records of the Miners' Union lodge at Hartley for the relevant period, but a search of the Minute Books of several other Miners' Lodges and Miners' Mutual Benefit Societies has revealed no hint that the sale of inscribed glasses was a way of raising money.

The Usworth Colliery Minute Book for the years 1889-1893 is typical and it provides us with a useful opportunity to relate surviving glasses to the records we have compiled. Six fatal accidents are mentioned in the Minute Book but the only person working at Usworth whose name we have seen recorded on a glass, *William Bell Boiler Explosion 11-4-91* (13) is not mentioned. The one employee, *John Graham* (76), who is mentioned and whose name also appears on a glass died in 1885, six months after an accident which occurred in 1884. His death certificate, recording death from natural causes, contradicts the inscription on the

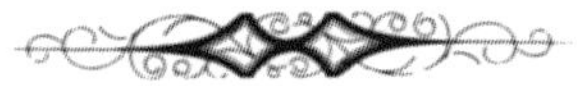

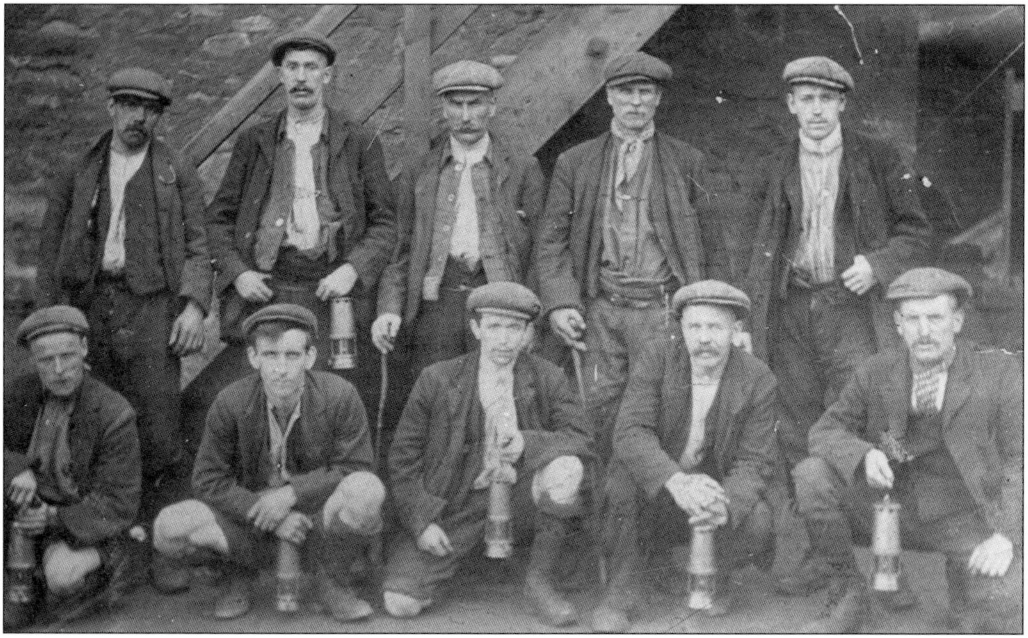

Gateshead Libraries & Arts

Gateshead miners around 1900.

glass which refers to an accident. If it were proved that the accident was not a prime cause of his death the mine's owners could not be held liable for compensation.

If the Miners' Union had any regular involvement in the production of these glasses why were more of these fatalities not recorded on glass? Further inscriptions may come to light but those we have seen so far reflect only a very small proportion of mine workers who died in accidents.

As well as the more important business of the colliery the Usworth book often minuted the trivia of miners' lives such as the purchase of a few yards of fringe for the bottom of the miners' banner. On another occasion it was 'Moved that a deputation wait upon Shanelly and his wife to see if they cannot get them to live peaceably together with their neighbours.' Charges were also agreed for miners' outings, suppers and concerts so if the glasses played a significant part in the provision of welfare or relief one might have expected to find a reference. Relief funds were established by mines for most of the major disasters and the miners' records report a variety of ways in which money was raised, such as concerts, football matches, theatre performances, etc. but nothing we have found mentions the sale of glassware.

There are, however, several other glasses relating to Usworth bearing inscriptions which could throw a different light on the reason for their creation. Three glasses relating to the explosion of 1885, are inscribed for named individuals – Barbara Meek, Mrs Night and J.J. Gordon. Since none of them matches any of those of the 42 men and boys who died in the explosion it seems reasonable to assume that the people named were not involved in the accident but had reason to want to remember it. It is more likely that they were commissioned privately, independent of any official miners' involvement.

We believe that the numbers of surviving glasses recording any particular disaster or accident must reflect in some degree the quantity originally produced, and that would have been influenced by the scale of the accident, the impact it made on the community at large and the demand for a memento of some kind. They may not represent production on a large scale for charitable purposes but could equally be a purely commercial operation to supply souvenirs. This may seem rather morbid to us today but death was an ever present fact of mining life.

There are other implications in the inscriptions on these glasses. If they were to help provide support for the dependents why do some of them record events relating to accidents in which men were not killed? A notable example relates to Robert Richardson (25), who was recovered alive after being entombed for 91 hours. If financial relief for the families was the primary objective his two companions who died in the tragedy would be worthier of remembrance. Possibly they were, but no glass recording their names has yet come to our

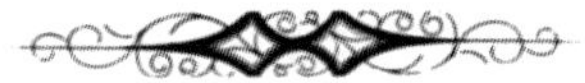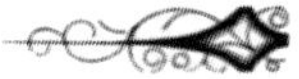

notice. The accident at Barrington Colliery, 1894 (15) was considered worthy of recording although no miner was injured. Then there are the other events and activities relating to mining that are also inscribed on glass. While it may be argued that glasses recording strikes (40-42) could have been sold for the relief of striking miners it is harder to apply that theory to those recording pay increases (45-46).

There are also items of glass that record several disasters separated by many years. A water jug in Beamish Museum commemorates the Seaham Colliery disaster of 1880, as well as the Washington disaster of 1908 and West Stanley 1909. Even if the last two events are close enough in time to be related to relief funds, the first event occurred nearly 30 years earlier. Without documentary evidence to link glasses directly to relief funds, the balance of probability is that they were produced either in quantity as commercial ventures to tap into the demand for souvenirs or were privately commissioned as mementoes for the members of grieving families.

There is some evidence that certain glasses were engraved as souvenirs of particular events in the mining industry and presented to individuals in appreciation of an act of bravery or a service rendered (see the Lambton Colliery glass, page 60). We have interviewed one gentleman whose grandfather was a member of a Mine Rescue Brigade. These brigades were made up of volunteers who attended accidents in their own pits and those nearby. He owns several glasses and is confident that they were presented to his grandfather and his fellow rescuers following their attendance at an accident.

Viewed as a whole the non-mining glasses can be divided into two groups, those that were probably made to be sold as souvenirs in commemoration of noteworthy local events and those that were commissioned by individuals or families to record personal events, usually deaths. The more one learns of the circumstances surrounding the events recorded on these glasses the more certain it appears that they are all part of a popular tradition that developed and flourished in the North East during the last quarter of the 19th century and the mining glasses should be seen as part of that tradition.

DATING THE GLASSES

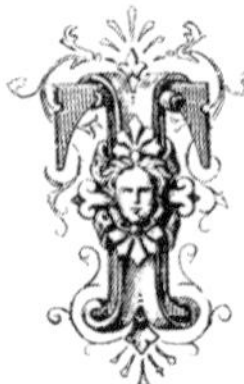he time-span of the dates on the glasses that we have recorded ranges from 1796 for the death of Robert Burns (113) to the Woodhorn Disaster in 1916 but the dates are not evenly spread over the period. Out of 130 different inscriptions there are no glasses bearing dates between 1863 (The Time Gun (70)) and 1879 (Jesse Ewen (71)) and only eight refer to events occurring before 1863. Of those, six relate to mining accidents and one to a miners' strike. None of them refers to the deaths of individuals and, apart from the Robert Burns glass, none has any connection with any event outside the North East.

Do these glasses relate to a North East tradition of recording events on glass? In 2006 an engraved goblet appeared in a London sale room. It refers to Lambton Colliery, north-east of Durham and one of the oldest collieries in the County. It has a bucket shaped bowl with two opposing handles and bears an engraved shield on one side containing the legend *R. Clark Engineer / Lambton Colliery / Presented by his / Gratefull Workmen / at Sunderland / November / 1848*. The reverse is engraved with a view of the pithead. The glass and inscription are undoubtedly contemporary with the date and the quality is typical of inscribed glass of the period. Whether this isolated example can be connected with the popular fashion for recording events on glass that emerged some 30 years later, however, is open to question.

Relating the pre-1863 accidents to the types of glass on which they appear, four of them (1-4) are on pub rummers, the dating of which we shall return to later, two (5-6) are recorded on several different types of glass,

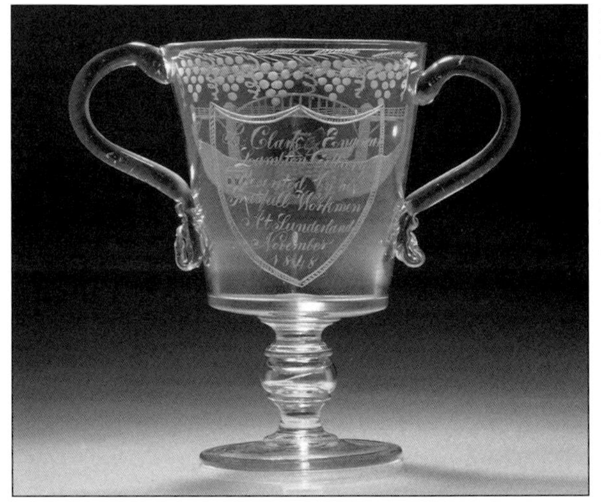

The Lambton glass. The hollow-knopped stem contains a silver threepenny piece. It is 22.4cm high.

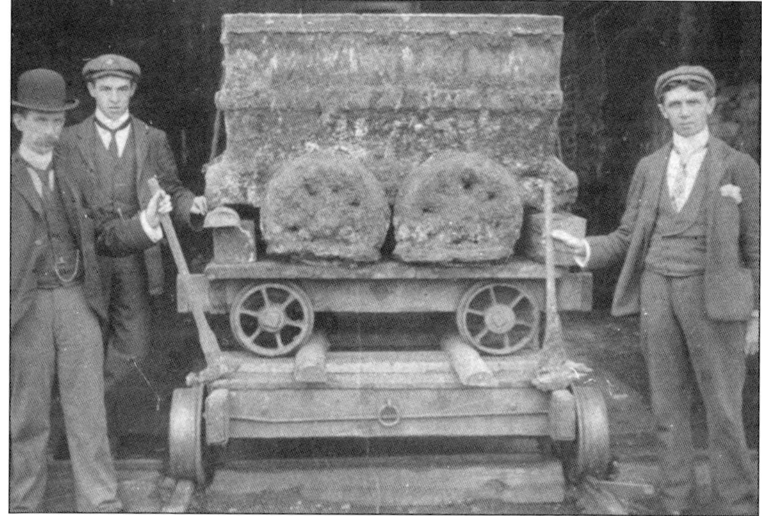

The Hartley Colliery disaster remained a poignant memory. This c1920 photograph shows an old tub from Hartley Colliery discovered during exploration of the abandoned workings dating to 1862.

including pub rummers, and one (5) is recorded twice, on a small pressed tankard and a thinly blown tumbler. While the dating of pub rummers may be open to discussion, the pressed tankards and the thin tumblers were certainly produced at the end of the 19th century and into the 20th century. Indeed, one of the small pressed tankards commemorating the Hartley disaster is inscribed in capital letters (a 20th century innovation). The chart on page 93 shows clearly that the majority of the glasses began to appear in 1880 and reached a peak between 1891 and 1895. Some of the glasses could not be contemporary with the pre-1870 events they commemorate and it is more likely that they were produced to mark anniversaries. The disaster at Haswell, 1844, would have had its 50th anniversary in 1894; Murton in 1898; Washington in 1901; Burradon and Hetton their 25th anniversaries in 1885 and Hartley in 1887. The centenary of the death of Robert Burns was in 1896. All these dates fall well within the period when most of the glasses were inscribed.

The one event prior to 1863, the beginning of the blank period on the chart, for which a number of glasses survive, is the Hartley Colliery disaster. This was probably the worst mining accident ever to happen in the North East and it seems reasonable that the idea for commemorating a tragedy on glass could have started at about that time. The advantage of doing this was that glass was a readily available medium that could easily be decorated by engraving. Without an inscribed date there is no way of placing an individual glass to a particular year but if a dated glass commemorating another event, say for an individual, should turn up that is contemporary with, or earlier than, the time of the Hartley disaster, then that raises the possibility that the Hartley glasses could have been produced continuously during the blank period on the chart. They would all bear the same date but might have been engraved in different years. It is difficult, otherwise, to find a logical explanation for not producing them on a regular basis until after 1880 unless, as suggested above, it was for the 25th anniversary as a form of remembrance at a time when the fashion for these glasses was firmly established. At this point we must introduce a cautionary note since we have second-hand information that some glasses commemorating the Hartley Colliery disaster have been made as copies in very recent times. Hartley glasses should therefore be viewed with caution.

Glasses recording the deaths of individuals occur regularly from 1880 onwards but we have so far recorded none for the blank period on the chart. This is strange since, although there were no major disasters, pit deaths were occurring just as regularly during that period as they did subsequently. Here are a few examples of the numbers of deaths recorded in the In Memoriam section kept by the Durham Mining Museum (www.dmm.org.uk) during the years 1863-1879. In Durham, Brancepeth Colliery, 16; East Hetton Colliery, 17; Usworth Colliery, 35. In Northumberland, Seghill Colliery, 22; Seaton Burn Colliery, 9; Burradon Colliery, 4.

Until glasses come to light that refer to events during this blank period we can only guess as to why the fashion for this type of commemorative ware only became popular after 1880. One possibility is that, if the first disaster glasses had been produced before 1880 as a consequence of the Hartley tragedy, the Seaham Colliery disaster of 1880, which almost equalled Hartley in loss of life, would have provided an equally valid reason to produce commemorative glass and thereby establish the practice of commemorating local tragedies. If this were the case it is feasible that they became familiar objects in the area so the idea was extended to include other less dramatic accidents and many other events, both public and private, as well as the anniversaries of long past events.

It is noticeable that for many years matters of local concern and interest dominate the inscriptions on the glasses and it is not until the onset of the Boer War at the end of the 19th century that matters of national concern start to appear on them. They may at first have been produced to reflect support for the many local men who went to South Africa and the vogue continued on the outbreak of World War I. Royalty is not mentioned until the death of Queen Victoria (120) in 1901. This may at first seem odd given the number of souvenirs that were produced for both the Queen's Golden and Diamond Jubilees but that market was more efficiently and artistically catered for by companies like George Davidson and Sowerby's Ellison Glassworks in Gateshead who produced masses of attractive, cheap pressed glass souvenirs to commemorate these events.

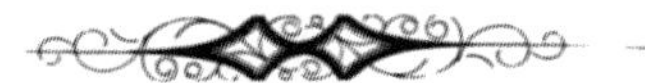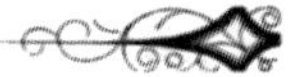

BUYERS AND MAKERS

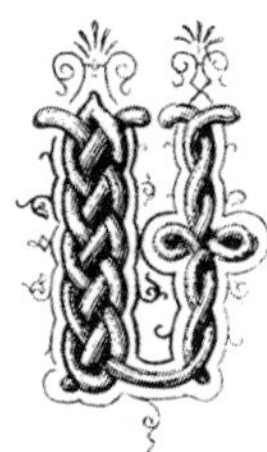ntil 1899, the inscriptions on the glasses refer almost exclusively to local events, working-class people, their employment and a few individuals well regarded in the local community. The majority of glasses relate, in one way or another, to the coal mining industry, mining accidents, and matters that closely affected the lives of miners. Glassmaking and shipbuilding were also important industries in the North East but, apart from the opening of the Albert Dock (74) which was probably seen more as a social occasion, neither is mentioned on any glass so far recorded.

J.B. Priestley experienced living conditions on the East Durham coalfield at first hand in 1933 and wrote, 'Your miner, then, is isolated, remote from the rest of the community, and generally in unpleasant surroundings, living in the beastliest towns and villages in the country … He sees little or nothing of you and me. On the other hand he sees a great deal of his fellow miners. They work together in an arduous and dangerous trade, in which they have to depend on one another for such safety as they have'. It seems reasonable that, in a close knit and self-reliant community, a practice that may have started casually as the result of a mine accident developed into a way of commemorating the trials and events of the mining community. The same means of expression seems then to have been adopted in the seafaring community around Blyth in Northumberland and, occasionally, with the general public as with John Findlater (79) in Newcastle upon Tyne.

The glasses come in a wide variety of shapes and styles but are generally unremarkable, small and of poor to moderate quality. The majority of the rummers are of soda glass and, if they were not produced locally, they could have been cheap imports from the continent. Other glassware, such as beer bottles, was certainly being imported in huge quantities into Newcastle at this time to the detriment of the local manufacturers. Items of pressed glass, which was an important manufacture in the area, were also inscribed. In addition to tumblers, jugs and sugar bowls bearing inscriptions, press-moulded tankards, in several sizes, became popular. We have seen one example of the smallest size inscribed Quarter Gill together with the excise mark and number for South Shields. This number was in use from 1879 to 1901 and it needs to be confirmed that the other sizes of similar tankards were of half gill and one gill capacity. During the period under review we have come across no instances of inscriptions on good quality glasses such as the Lambton Colliery glass or the Sunderland

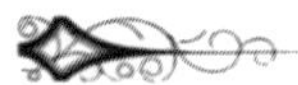 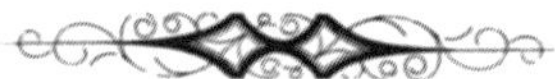

Bridge goblets, of the first half of the 19th century. Perhaps the best quality objects we have seen are straight-sided water jugs that sometimes commemorate two or three of the major disasters. It is hard to believe that any of the drinking glasses could have ever been regarded by visitors from further afield as suitable souvenirs of a visit to the North East. It must have been the message rather than the medium that was important and this places them firmly as very personal mementoes of a working-class community remembering their own.

The problem of dating the pub rummers that were regularly used for the inscriptions has yet to be satisfactorily resolved. The two commonest shapes have either round bowls or straight-sided flat-bottomed bowls. There is no doubt, from the dates on them, that they were in general use from at least 1880 to around the time of the First World War but establishing just how early they came into use is not so easy. Many of them have a distinctive 'T' or 'Y' mark under the foot which results from the method of manufacture and is generally accepted to indicate that they were produced no earlier than the late 19th century.

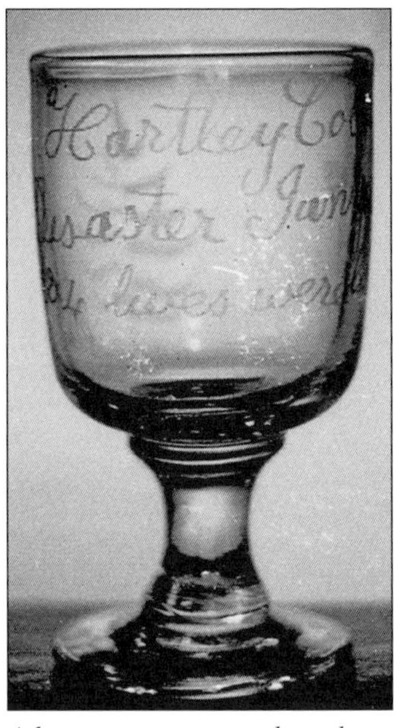

A large rummer remembers the Hartley Colliery disaster.

The quality of the engraving on the glasses is often coarse and at best mediocre and there are sometimes mistakes in spelling, as in NOW WEE SHANT BE LONG (51), and inaccuracies in the transcription of names and dates. The latter is interesting since it brings into question the literacy of both the engraver and whoever commissioned the glass. The discrepancy in the recording of the names Noble/Nobley (60) is a case in point, the former appearing in newspaper reports while the latter, which is correct, generally appears on glasses. Dates and ages recorded sometimes disagree slightly with the public record as in *James Newton* (104) who was recorded on the glass as *aged 98 years* and died on October 1 whereas the registrar recorded him as 96 and dying on October 2. The greatest discrepancy in a name occurs on the *Sarah Corbitt* glass (80). The name on the glass can be read in several ways but Corliff would be a fair interpretation. Research shows that her name was almost certainly Corbitt. The *Lord Walkworth* (sic) (Warkworth) (97) glass is another

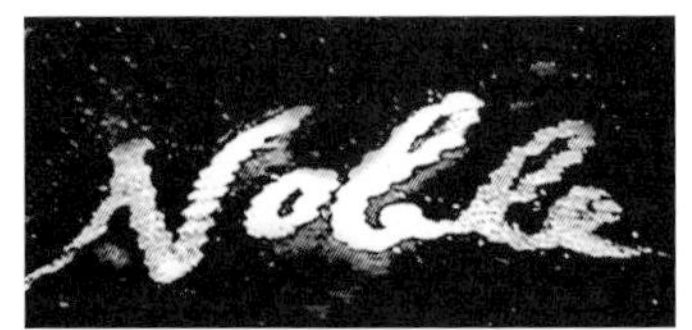

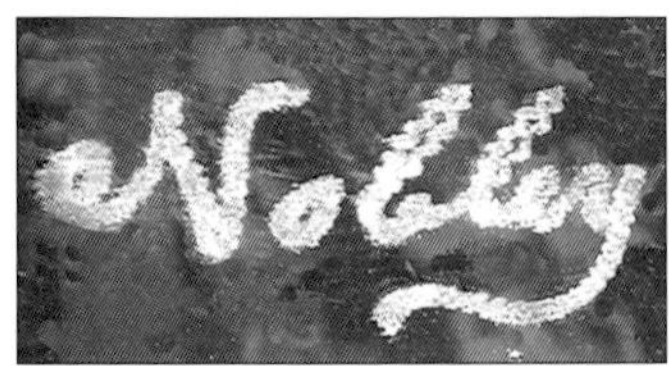

good example. Why were these errors accepted unless those who commissioned the glasses had given the engraver the wrong information or were unable to read? Literacy was by no means universal in these communities at this time and contemporary death certificates not infrequently show witnesses signing with a cross.

These points may help us to understand who did the engraving and who bought the glasses when there was already a long tradition of good quality engraving on glass in the North East. Collectors will be familiar with Sunderland Bridge rummers, made and sold as souvenirs from the time of the opening of the bridge in 1796 to about 1850, and there are several very fine locally engraved goblets bearing other subjects in the Laing Art Gallery in Newcastle and Sunderland Museum. It seems likely that the people who inscribed the disaster glasses were not highly accomplished engravers but might have been employed as decorators in the glass factories.

Having established that they were produced over a period of about 30 years it becomes obvious that there must have been a number of engravers at work and a more detailed study of the inscriptions bears this out.

There are several aspects of the inscriptions to consider when trying to identify individual engravers. The most significant of these is the calligraphy, particularly the way in which some of the upper case letters are formed. Peculiarities of spelling recur and probably indicate the same hand at work on different glasses. Many glasses are ornamented with a decorative motif and these also vary. Perhaps even the wording of the inscription may point to a particular engraver.

Some of the principal differences and characteristics we have noted are illustrated below but we would need to study many more of these glasses to determine how many of these distinguishing features may be peculiar to a particular engraver.

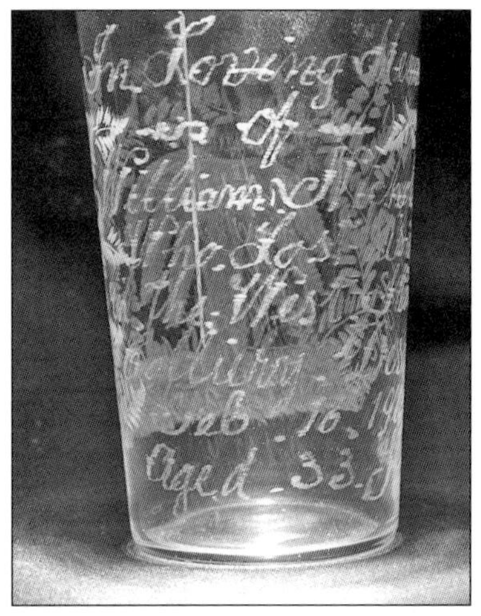

This tumbler (35) remembers William Nicholson who lost his life in the West Stanley Colliery disaster, 1909.

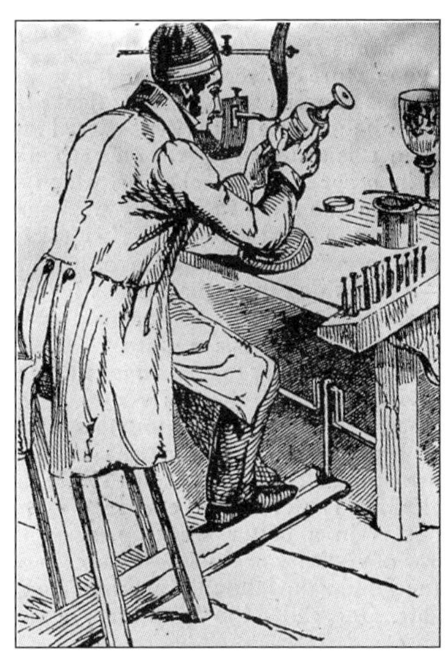

An engraver uses a treadle-powered machine

Authors' collection

SOME DETAILS

The inscription on many of the glasses commences with *In Memory of* … and there are distinctive differences in the way the capital M is formed. is the most common is an obvious capital with a cursive stroke at the beginning but in another form it appears as a larger version of a lower case 'm'.

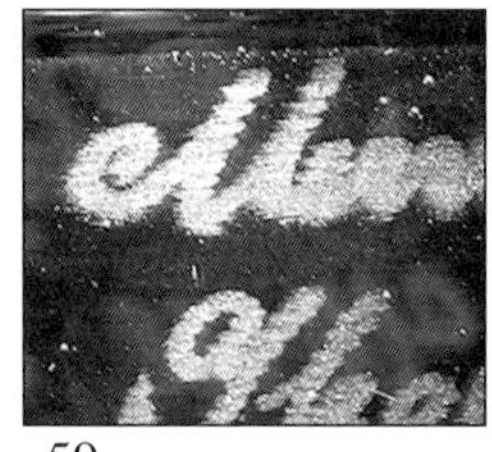

59

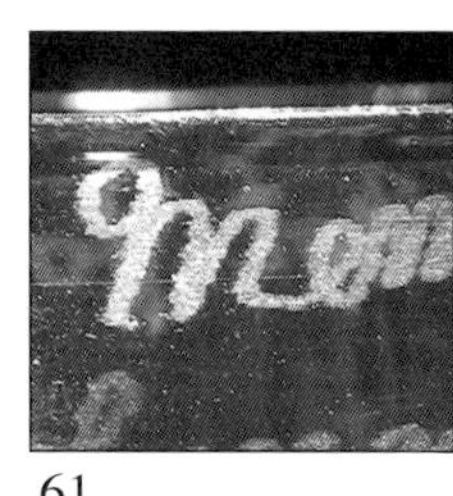

61

The capital letter B has two distinct forms. In one case a short upwards line leads to the top of the vertical stroke. In another a flourish like a lower case 'a' introduces the letter. This peculiarity may also be seen on other letters and numbers (see below).

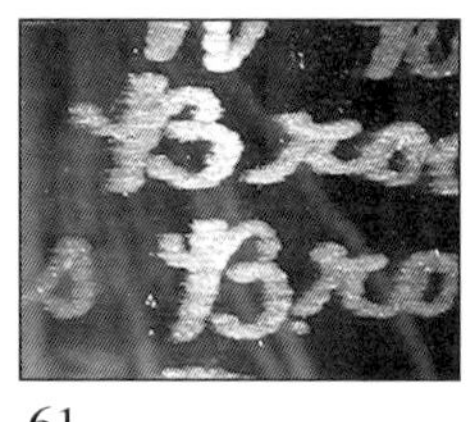

61

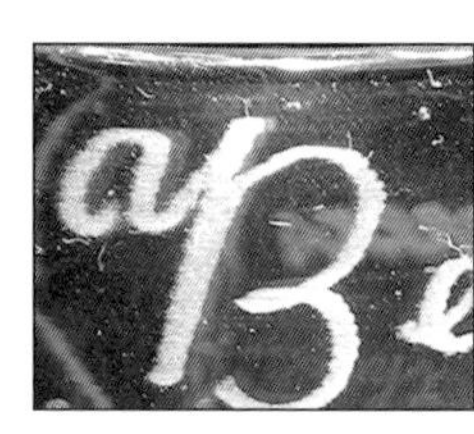

68

One regularly re-occurring characteristic is the flourish at the beginning of the letters in this group. *John Henry Todd* (59), *Andrew Scott* (94), both 1894, *Charles Fenwick* (105) 1895. At its most distinctive it looks like a lower case 'a'. The same flourish also appears on the 7 of 1897 on the Kelloe glass (22).

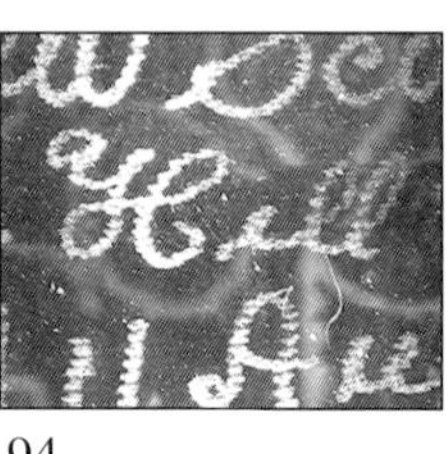

94

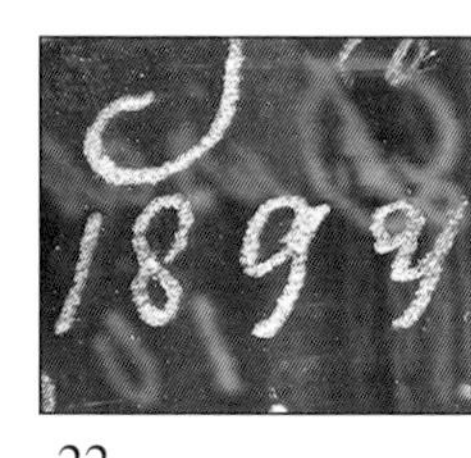

22

A number of glasses, all cut with a rather wide wheel, spell *Success* in the 17th century style with the first 's' resembling an f. Among them are, *Success to Hartford* (50), *Success to Prospect Terrace Amble* (107), *In Honour of Lord Walkworth* (97) and *Success to Charles Fenwick MP*, (105) all dated 1895 and it is idiosyncrasies such as this that, we believe, points to glasses being engraved by the same individual.

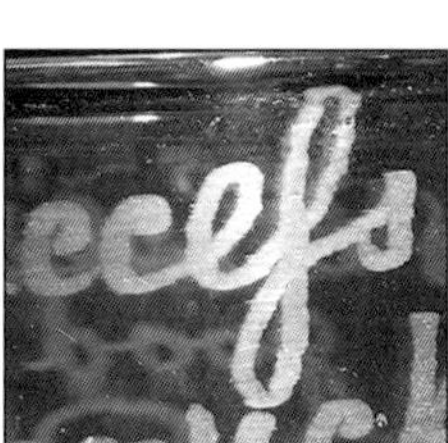

105

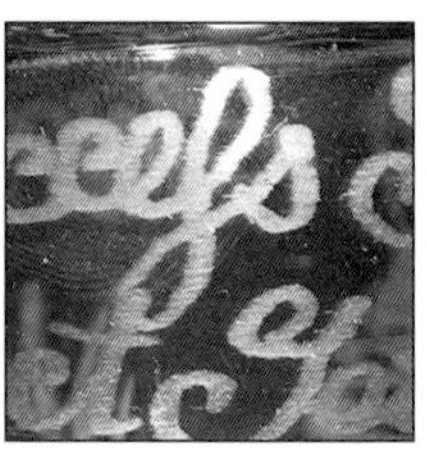

107

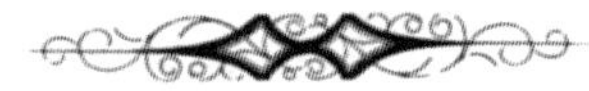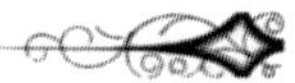

Some of the glasses relating to drowning or shipping accidents, particularly those relating to Blyth, bear engravings of boats. This suggests a more competent engraver than those who decorated many of the glasses relating to coalmining.

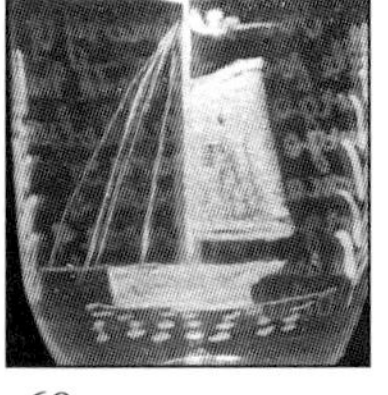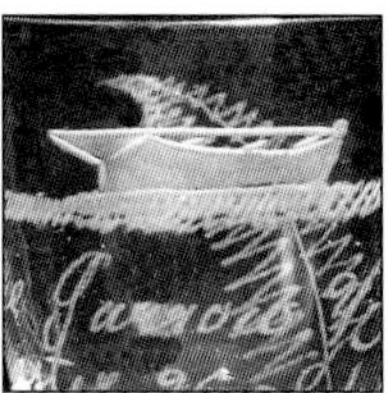

60

62

The most distinctively different style of engraving is in the use of capital letters throughout. This form is found almost exclusively in commemoration of events occurring in or after 1912. The sinking of the *Titanic* (1912) (127), the *Lusitania* (1915) (130) and the several examples relating to disasters at West Stanley (1909) (34) and Woodhorn (1916) (39) are commemorated in this way. One glass (128) is unusual with an inscription commemorating the start of World War I executed in capitals and in cursive script.

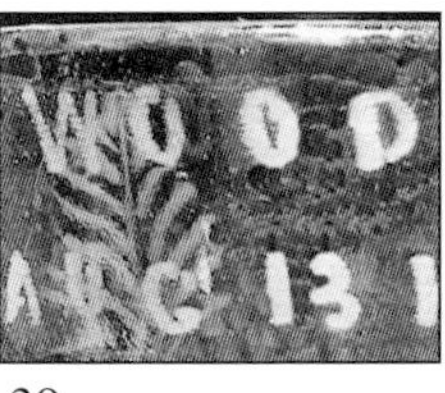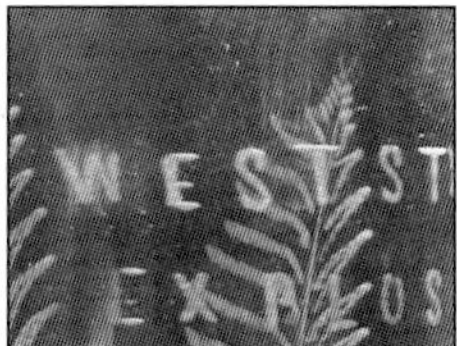

39

34

An idiosyncrasy that identifies another engraver is the liberal use of full stops between the words, for example: *A Present . To . Kate . Lumsdon . In . Memory . Of . William . Old . Who . Lost . his. Life . At . Craghead . Colliery* (14). The script, more elegant than that on many glasses, is characteristic and is replicated with full stops on another generous tumbler and two jugs.

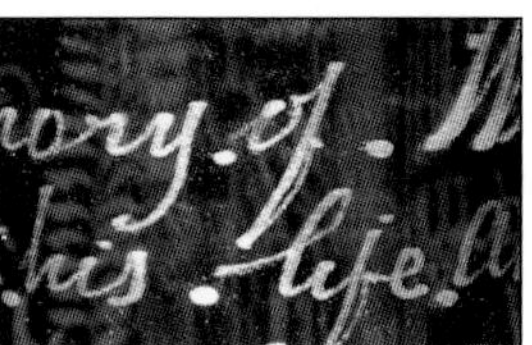

14

A distinctive technique appears on a number of glasses dated 1910-11 which must be the work of the same engraver. The capital letters of the glasses commemorating the Whitehaven Disaster (37), Bolton Explosion (38) and Coronation of George V (124) are all embellished with distinctive added flourishes.

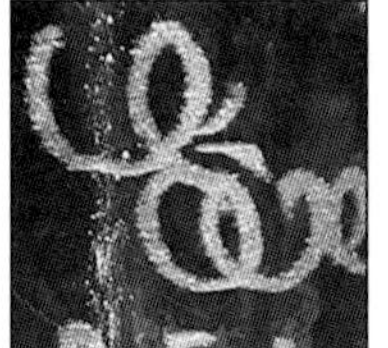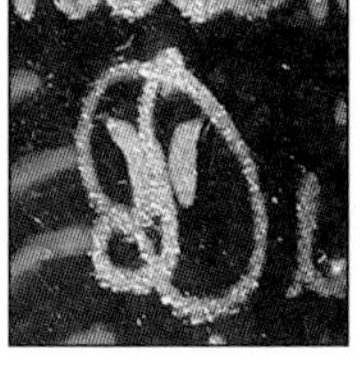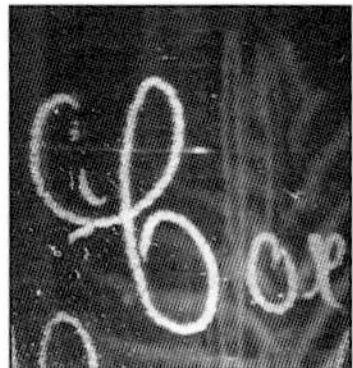

38

37

124

A characteristic seen on glasses commemorating the death of King Edward VII and the coronation of King George V is the form of capital Ks that bear some resemblance to a capital H. This peculiarity is also found on the Kelloe Colliery glass of 1897 (22) and a glass engraved *Keep off The Black List* (55). A

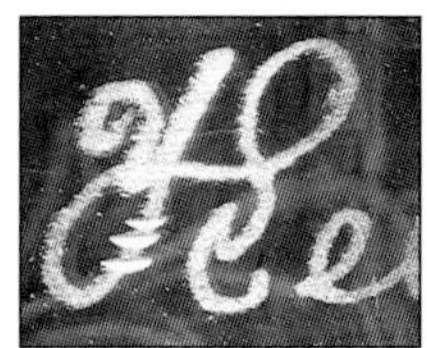

22

'black list' of individuals suspected of promoting industrial disputes and strikes was circulated among mine owners in both the 19th and 20th centuries, perhaps as early as the 1840s. The Black List glass is undated but the capital K places it, with some certainty, between the very end of the 19th and the early years of the 20th century.

A clover leaf is a common decorative motif on the reverse of the glasses. Most have minimal or no ornamentation and the left hand leaf appears to start from the top of the stem and is drawn in a clockwise direction. Others are flanked by spiral scrolls and the left leaf is drawn in an anti-clockwise direction.

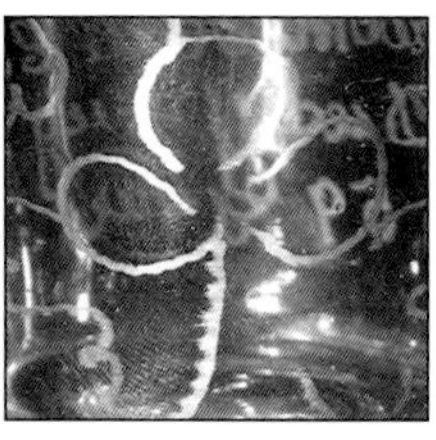

92

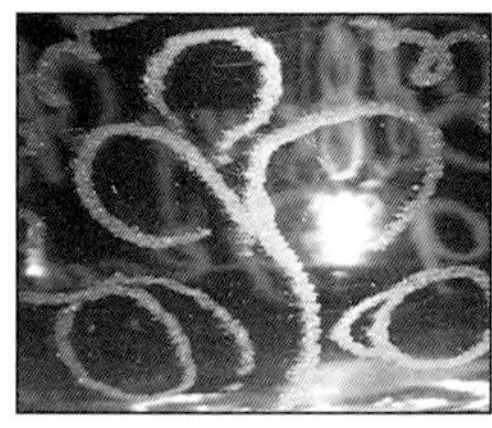

93

Mistakes in spelling such as *Lost there* [sic] *lives, an* (sic) *boiler explosion* and *They* [sic] *will be done'* lead us to suspect that the engravers were either not very well educated or were less than meticulous in their recording. Occasionally there are repetitions of mis-spelling that suggest they are specific to one engraver. The Charles Fenwick (105) glass includes 'he' spelled as 'hee'. This peculiarity also occurs on NOW WEE SHANT BE LONG (50) although the first is in cursive script while the latter is in capital letters. Did the engraver change his style? However, the variation in the recording of the number of deaths in disasters can be explained by the engraving of glasses before the final death toll was established.

The North East was probably not alone in producing engraved glasses commemorating events of national concern. There are, for instance, many variations on the subject of the Boer War (always called the Transvaal War) and it could be argued that, since this was an event of national interest, glasses commemorating the war could have been produced anywhere in the country, and probably were.

The general standard of engraving on commemorative and souvenir glass produced in other glassmaking areas such as Lancashire and Birmingham is normally executed to a higher standard. We illustrate one example inscribed *A Present from Birmingham*.

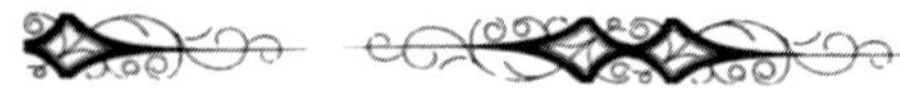

We believe that the glasses we have listed fit all the criteria for North Eastern glass. It is also clear from this group that a particular event could attract the attention of more than one engraver. *Transvaal War Commenced* (115) and *Transvaal War Three cheers for General White* (116), for instance, are obviously engraved by different hands, differing both in wheel thickness and in the style of the capital Ts and Ws.

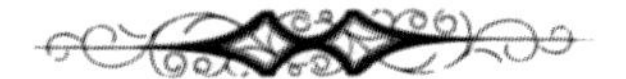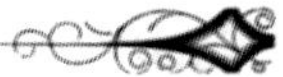

This suggests that when a wider public interest was involved several engravers were inscribing glasses for general sale to take advantage of the popular mood of patriotism.

The form of words used may also point to an individual engraver. While most glasses confine themselves to the basic facts a few carry inscriptions which contain words that qualify those facts such as *An Alarming Accident* (15), *Mystery solved* (30), *Serious fire* (49). This was how the accidents were reported in newspaper headlines and suggest someone with a little more imagination who wanted his work to make an impact, particularly if the glasses were being offered to the general public.

With one exception all the glasses we have recorded are wheel engraved. That exception is a jug, poorly inscribed in diamond point, with a view of the pithead, that commemorates the West Stanley disaster. It is most likely the work of an amateur executed for his own purposes. It does make the point, however, that the practice of commemorating these events on glass was widespread. One final point is that engravers did not limit themselves to working on one style of glass. Two glasses commemorating the Whitehaven disaster, a wine glass and a miniature tumbler, are clearly engraved by the same person.

Some of the glasses were presented for services rendered, like those given to members of colliery rescue brigades, and we have also had some of our speculations confirmed by local residents. Many of the glasses have a fairground character and quality and one can imagine them being engraved and sold as souvenirs at local shows and fairs. Glasses inscribed as being *A Present from* … also suggest that they may have been impulse buys at a public event.

There is strong evidence that not all engravers were confined to workshops or shops and that itinerant engravers worked both in and outside the North East. John Brooks has identified the work of one such engraver from recording about 20 glasses engraved over a 25 year period from about 1850 onwards that were undoubtedly executed by the same hand. They refer to people and places around the coast from Newcastle to Southampton and the consistent style of engraving and the coastal connection strongly suggests an engraver travelling regularly by ship around the East and South coasts. Some of these glasses also have decoration linking them stylistically to the Newcastle-Sunderland area and all are engraved with both wheel and diamond point by a competent hand. This is not to imply that this worker was responsible for any of the glasses that are the subject of this book but to make the point that glass engraving was pursued as an itinerant business at that time.

We spoke to a local resident whose grandfather was a mining engineer at Sacriston colliery. He had four daughters and one day, in about 1895 she believes, an itinerant engraver came to the house and, using a treadle-powered wheel, he engraved four pub rummers, one for each girl, with their name and the year. At least one of these glasses survives. If this was a general practice it would help to explain why we have seen glasses that bear only a name and a date that does not appear to relate to any significant event in their life.

Local events and public occasions that drew large crowds, such as the opening of Holywell Bridge (93), Seaton Sluice Bridge (90) or the laying of the foundation stone of Ashington Miners' Hall (47), provided good opportunities for an itinerant engraver to ply his trade. Lasting souvenirs of the event could be acquired at the site and on the day.

We have also seen glasses bought at major exhibitions around the country that, as well as recording the

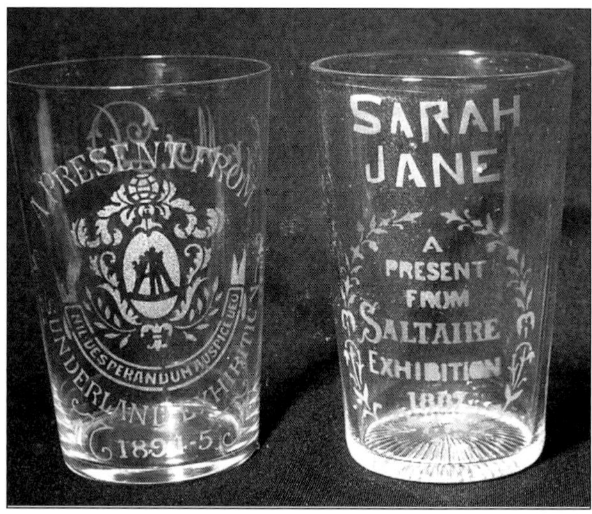

exhibition, (such as Glasgow, Edinburgh, Sunderland, Saltaire (above)) were also engraved with the name of the purchaser.

Even if the glasses produced in the North East were commonly sold at fairs, some of the engravers must have had more permanent premises to which the public had access. A death in the family could be remembered in this way and the glasses were likely to have been commissioned from an engraver by the family for distribution at or immediately after the funeral. As it might have been impractical to wait for the next fair or gala, it is likely that there were shops or business premises where people could place orders, either directly with the engraver or with a middle man.

Some of the biggest shows in the North East were the annual Miners' Galas and we feel that an engraver who would commemorate one type of event, say a boxing match (68) or a hanging (67), at an ordinary fair or market could easily set up a booth with an engraving machine at a Miners' Gala to commemorate any mining-related event. One of our informants, a lady, reports that her grandfather bought glasses at the Durham Miners' Gala on three successive years. They were inscribed *Durham Miners' Strike 1892*, *Its Very Canny 1893* and *Better Luck to the Durham Miners 1894*.

It is clear that there were a number of engravers but who were they? They were likely to be associated with the glass industry since most glass houses employed engravers. Some, as we have noted, were skilled artists but the pressed glass firms also employed engravers to apply simple decoration such as ferns and floral sprays to cheap pressed glass. This country has a long tradition of cottage industry and the glass industry was no exception. Craftsmen

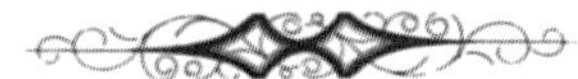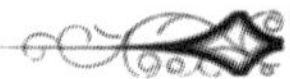

often set up facilities in their homes or back yards to supplement their incomes by doing, out of hours, what they were employed to do at the factory; this was called crib work. The engraving machines could be treadle operated (see page 65) so it would not be difficult to set up a workshop at home.

Towards the end of the 19th century there was considerable competition from continental imports which affected the main glass producing areas of England. If employees of the glass industry were being laid off it is likely that individuals with suitable skills might try their luck as freelance engravers.

After examining and comparing more than 250 of these glasses we can suggest that:

• engravers might be either itinerant or working from permanent premises.

• a number of engravers were responsible for the glasses but most were not highly skilled or well educated.

• events were recorded by more than one engraver.

• an engraver might work on more than one type of glass.

• significant anniversaries of earlier events were commemorated.

• glasses commemorating the major disasters and public events were most likely made in large numbers as souvenirs to be sold by way of normal retail trade.

• while the fashion lasted, glasses were also commissioned in small numbers by individuals to mark personal tragedies or specific achievements.

• The period during which these glasses were produced covered the years 1880-1915.

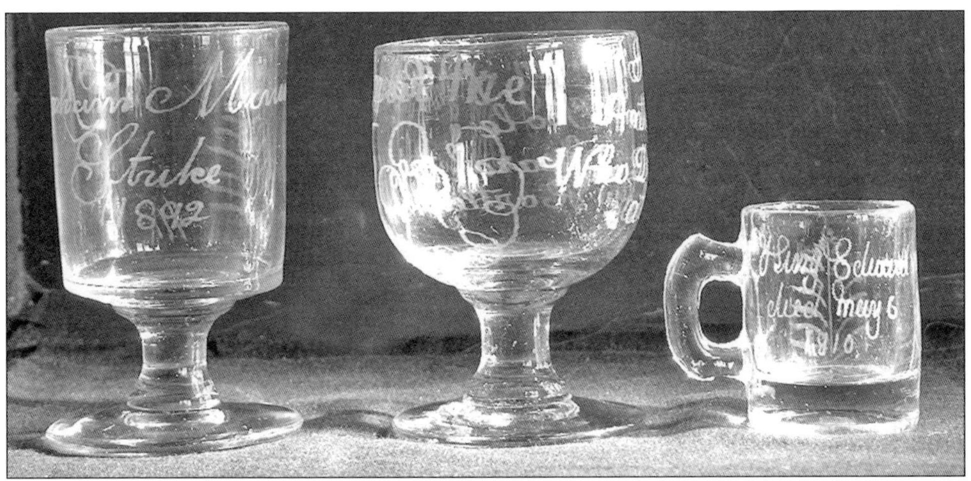

Without doubt there are more inscriptions to be found and more tales to be told and it would be particularly interesting if a glass should come to light that can be dated with confidence either to the blank period on our chart (1863-1879) or earlier. If, as a result of this book, such evidence comes to light then our efforts will have been well rewarded.

DECORATIONS AND ADDITIONAL PHRASES

The reverse sides of glasses are frequently decorated with ferns, either vertical or diagonal or somewhat less frequently with clover leaves or with vaguely stylised flowers. Other devices seen have included Union flags, a yacht, a rowing boat, a palm tree and a pit head. The following phrases have been recorded, usually, but not always on the reverse:

Accidents will happen
auld Lang Syne
Come for all things are now ready
Gone but not Forgotten
Hee's [sic] *a Jolly good fellow*
Hold the Fort for l Am Coming
In the midst of Life We are in death
In the Sweet by and by
Not a day to call our own
Not forgotten
0 think of The home over there
Remember Me
Rock of ages
Rock of Ages cleft for Me
Safe in the arms of Jesus
Shall we meet beyond the river
Still in memory
Suffer the children to come to Me
Thy will be done

The use of upper and lower case letters has been preserved

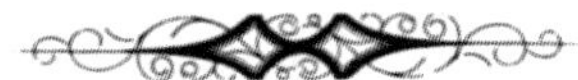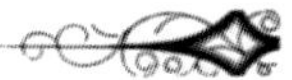

THE NORTH EAST COALFIELD

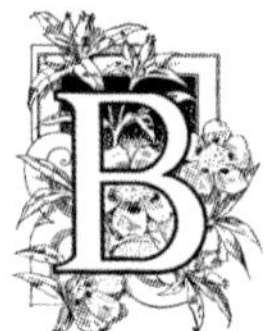By the mid-13th century sea coal was being collected along the Northumberland coast to be used by smiths and lime burners. It was soon realised that the loose coal on the surface came from seams running into the ground so people started digging in open pits.

Mining flourished and Newcastle became a wealthy town with much of its coal output being shipped to London. It had been thought that as mines reached the water table production would become impossible and the use of coal as a fuel would come to an end. However there was a great incentive to overcome the problem and methods of drainage were developed that allowed shafts to be driven into the deeper coal seams. The earliest system of drainage collected water in a sump from which it was lifted by an endless chain carrying buckets driven by manpower. As shafts went deeper horses were employed to drive the chain but there was a limit to the distance over which water could be lifted so several chains were installed to lift the water by stages. Matters improved when watertight linings, known as coffering, were introduced in the late 17th century, and the advent of the Newcomen steam engine and pump in 1710 provided the first mechanical power which enabled mines to be drained to a greater depth. With the mines deeper and drier, the next problems to arise were those of ventilation and firedamp.

An ever-present danger of deep mining was the the inflammable gas, methane, that issued from the rock strata. Strong currents of this gas were termed 'blowers'. Methane, so-called 'firedamp', burns in air to produce carbon dioxide and water and miners could suffer burns when 'blowers' ignited. However, if the mine was inadequately ventilated and oxygen not plentiful a different chemical reaction took place and the methane

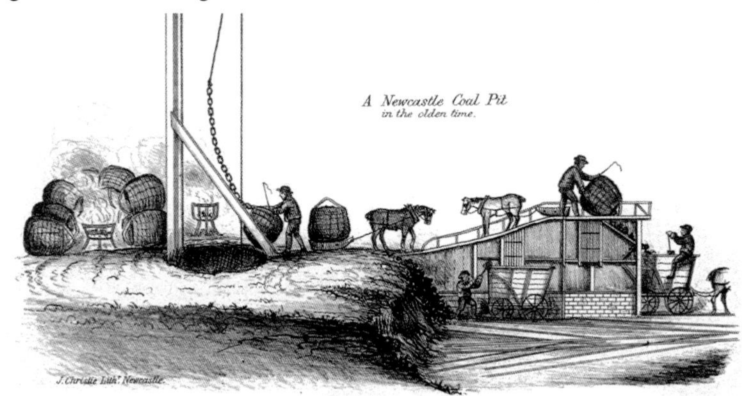

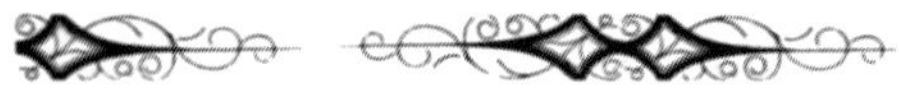

burned to produce not only carbon dioxide and water but, most dangerously, carbon monoxide (the dreaded 'afterdamp'). Thus carbon monoxide poisoning was a major cause of death following ignition of firedamp. Ignition

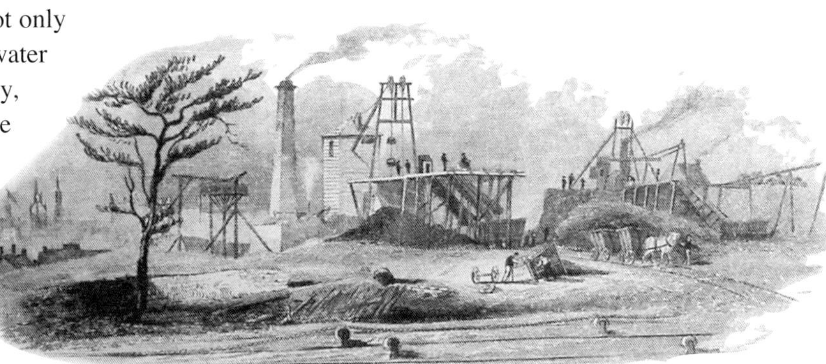

Picton Main Colliery.

could be caused by naked flames such as the candles used by miners before the introduction of safety lamps or by the firing of shots, (controlled explosions) to clear rock.

Because of the expense of sinking deeper shafts to follow the coal seams, the tendency was to sink fewer shafts of larger diameter containing both the pumping and winding mechanisms. This in turn led to problems with the dispersal of gas which was the cause of so many major accidents. Two shafts provided a down draught and an up draught and the most effective way, used for many years, to induce a draught through the mine was to have a fire associated with the up-shaft. This worked while the flow of fire damp was moderate and could be burned off regularly in the workings, but large and sudden outbursts of gas sometimes got as far as the fire causing major explosions. As mines got deeper and the gas problem became worse, the most successful method of ventilation was use of suction fans placed over the up draught

Advances in iron smelting during the 18th century led to better cast iron, which in turn led to the manufacture of more powerful steam engines and, hence, more efficient mining. By the end of the 18th century wooden 'tubbing' was replaced by cast iron for lining pit shafts, and iron rails replaced the wooden ones used for moving coal trucks both underground and from the pithead to the coal wharves

Newcomen steam engines were still being used to pump water from the mines but coal was raised by horses operating a form of windlass. The first attempt to use the steam engine to raise coal was made at Hartley Colliery in 1763, but it was not considered satisfactory. However, when Watts developed his double-acting steam engine in 1794, steam power could successfully be applied directly to the winding mechanism and this rapidly became the standard method of raising coal.

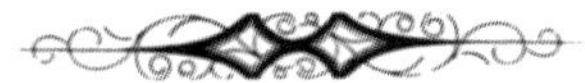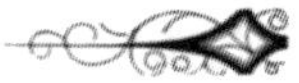

Lighting was always a problem in the mines and the dangers of a naked flame were only too frequently demonstrated. A crude form of lighting, considered to be safer than a naked flame was achieved with a disc of iron called a steel mill. Made to revolve at high speed, it produced a stream of sparks when a flint was pressed against it. Although widely used, it still caused a number of explosions and where the danger of firedamp was particularly strong it was not unknown for miners to work in total darkness.

The progress towards safer lighting started in 1811 when Dr Clanny produced the first safety lamp but it was not very well received. However, it did highlight the continuing problem of serious accidents. New lamps were produced, at more or less the same time, by George Stephenson and Sir Humphry Davy. With safer lighting now available, old mines which had been abandoned as too dangerous to work were reopened, more coal became accessible to the hewers in existing mines and output increased dramatically because of better visibility.

The traditional way of raising coal to the surface was in wicker baskets called corves which carried 5-6 cwt. These were attached to a rope and hung free without guiding or controlling mechanism. Because they were free to swing against the shaft side, descending empty corves often caused snags. This was overcome by putting a wooden dividing wall, called a brattice, between ascending and descending corves. Eventually these brattices were enlarged to create separate shafts for pumping, ventilation and the corves. Miners descended the shaft in the coal corves and it was apparently normal for the boys to travel up and down by clinging to the rope between the baskets.

The first attempt to improve upon these methods was the installation of iron tubs at South Hetton colliery in 1833. Safety was further improved when cages were introduced to carry the miners up and down the shaft and the wooden shaft linings were replaced by iron guide rails and steadies on the cage. All these improvements slowly provided a safer means of transport for the miners.

Conditions continued to improve in mines in spite of the conservatism of both coal owners and miners. The first attempts to introduce electricity took place about 1882 and coal cutting machinery gradually led to the replacement of hand cutting. Improvements to the winding gear led to a reduction in the number of accidents in the pit shafts and higher qualifications were required for mining engineers.

Moves for better regulation of mining grew as the continuous stream of 'minor' accidents involving the loss of one or several lives totalled more than the losses in major disasters. This was attributed to wide variations in the quality of management and operation of mines, thus increasing the call for regulation. In 1850 the first Mines Act was passed for a period of five years. It was renewed for a further five and at the end of that period became permanent. The

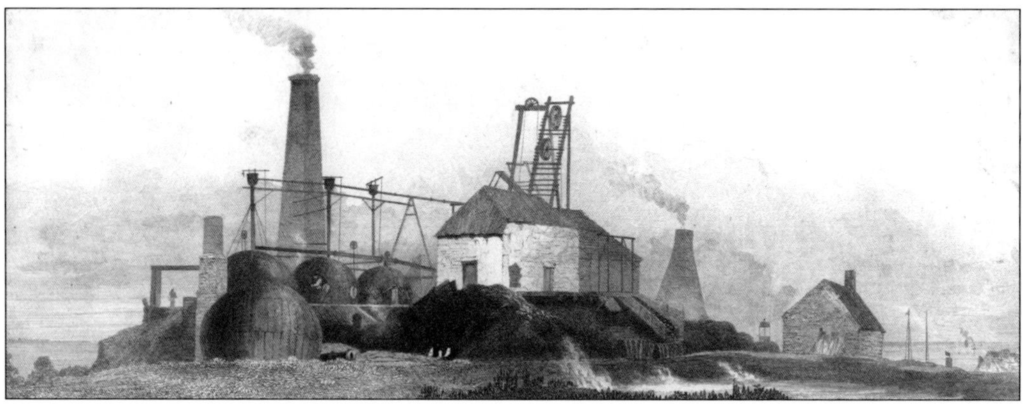

Hartley Colliery, engraved by Newcastle artist Thomas Hair in the 1840s.

North of England Institute of Mining and Mechanical Engineers was opened in Newcastle in 1852.

Accidents continued to occur far too frequently and for a long time it was believed there existed a conspiracy between the coal owners and the newspapers to restrict the way they were reported. However, the publicity created by the development of the safety lamp finally increased public awareness of the constant loss of life, and organisations concerned with safety in the mines came into being during the 19th century. Lobbying of parliament produced the first public inquiry into the state of mining in 1835. Within three months it had presented its findings but they were not considered specific enough to warrant legislation. In 1843 a committee in the North East recommended that no new mine should be opened without having two shafts but it was not until after the Hartley Colliery disaster in 1862 that this was made law. This committee also suggested that there should be a government inspectorate of mines as there already was for the railways.

Towards the end of the 19th century it was suspected that coal dust itself was an explosive and that the carbon in coal dust could burn explosively to yield both carbon monoxide and dioxide and was the probable cause of several disasters. The Atkinson brothers, inspectors of mines, had published a book, *Explosions in Coal Mines* drawing attention to this highly dangerous hazard. Some coal owners tried to have the book suppressed but by the beginning of the 20th century the danger was accepted as real and attempts were made to mitigate it by scattering non-inflammable stone dust in the roadways.

Despite these advances, mining remained a dangerous occupation; between 1880 and 1910 there were more than 1,000 deaths every year in British mines.

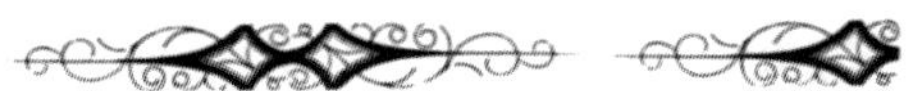

THE NORTH EAST GLASS TRADITION

he earliest evidence of glassmaking in the North East of England is provided by the late 7th century writer, the Venerable Bede. He recorded that, in 675, the bishop of Monkwearmouth brought glassmakers from Gaul to glaze his new abbey but there is no evidence that glassmaking continued after this task was completed.

Glassmaking returned to the Newcastle area on a commercial basis as a consequence of several patents taken out between 1610 and 1615 aimed at replacing wood with coal as the only fuel in industrial furnaces. By the time that the use of wood was finally banned in 1615, Sir Robert Mansell, Vice-Admiral of the navy, had become the holder of these patents and, as a consequence, became the owner of a considerable monopoly. Mansell was not a glassmaker so his business strategy was to license glassmakers for the use of coal and then dictate what they could make and where they could sell it. The principal market for both coal and glass was London and it made sense, therefore, to set up glasshouses close to the source of fuel and a good supply route to London. Newcastle met both these criteria; the cost of transporting glass overland from Nottinghamshire glasshouses to London was twice as expensive as shipping it by sea from Newcastle. Glassmaking in England (mainly window glass and bottles) had always been In the hands of foreign craftsmen who jealously guarded their skills so the first glass makers, with a licence from Mansell, to arrive in the Newcastle area in about 1620 were descendants of those immigrant Huguenot glass workers who had come to England from Normandy and Lorraine during the 16th century to escape religious persecution. By the time Mansell's monopoly ended in 1642, when his patents were revoked by Parliament, they had firmly established the manufacture of window glass and bottles near the River Tyne around the Ouseburn where their descendants continued to prosper.

The late 17th century saw the introduction of a new trade in domestic table glass made from the newly developed lead crystal glass (generally referred to as 'flint glass') and the first glasshouse to produce it in the North East was established in 1684 by the Dagnia family in the Closegate outside the west wall of the city. In 1696 Houghton's letters, describing the state of various industries in England, recorded 11 glasshouses in Newcastle upon Tyne. The 18th century saw the establishment of several other flint glass houses in the Closegate; among them Airey Cookson & Co., all producing domestic table glass for the local market and for

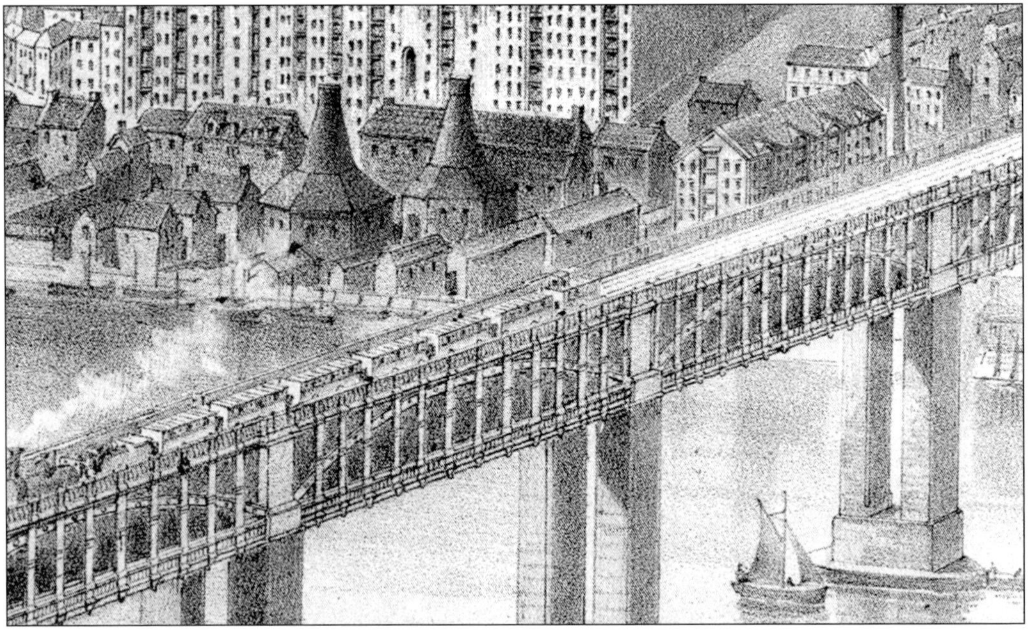

The conical chimneys of Closegate Bottleworks on the banks of the Tyne, established in 1684. Domestic glassware was in demand from the 17th century. They are pictured here around 1860 by artist John Storey.

export to Europe. During the 19th century, however, continental glassmakers were quicker than those in Newcastle to take advantage of technical improvements to furnaces and glassmaking methods. Glassmaking on the Tyne and Wear suffered as a consequence. By the 1880s continental makers were delivering bottles for the beer trade to Newcastle breweries that were better and cheaper than could be brought from the local glasshouses. The efforts of the glasshouse owners to reduce costs led to a year-long strike in 1882-83 and, by the end of it, the number of bottle glass houses had fallen from 13 to three. In contrast to this reluctance in some quarters to change old habits, firms such as Sowerby and George Davison quickly adopted a new glassmaking process that arrived in the North East during the second half of the 19th century via Birmingham and Manchester. This was the machine moulding of glass, usually called press-moulding, which had first come to England from the USA during the 1830s. After almost all other types of glassmaking had disappeared in the North East, moulded glass continued until the 1930s. The last working glasshouse in Newcastle was Rush's Bridge Works.

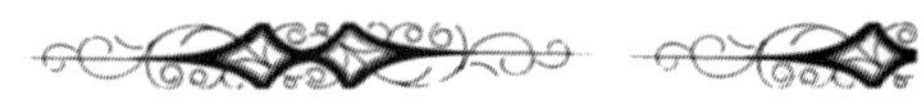

TABLES OF GLASSES AND INSCRIPTIONS

The following tables list all the inscriptions that we have found up to the time of publication together with the date of the event and, where applicable, a reference to published sources where anyone interested may find a fuller account than we have been able to give in the narrative. Much information relating to accidents and disasters in North Eastern coal mines can be found on the Durham Mining Museum website at www.dmm.org.uk.

The letter in the final column relates to the key below which indicates, wherever possible, what type of glass the inscription was found on.

Key

A   Pub glass with rounded bowl
B   Pub glass with straight parallel sides and flat-bottomed bowl
C   Small tumbler
D   Large tumbler
E   Small tankard
F   Large tankard
G   Wine glass
H   Bowl
I   Press Moulded Jug
J   Blown jug
K   Other

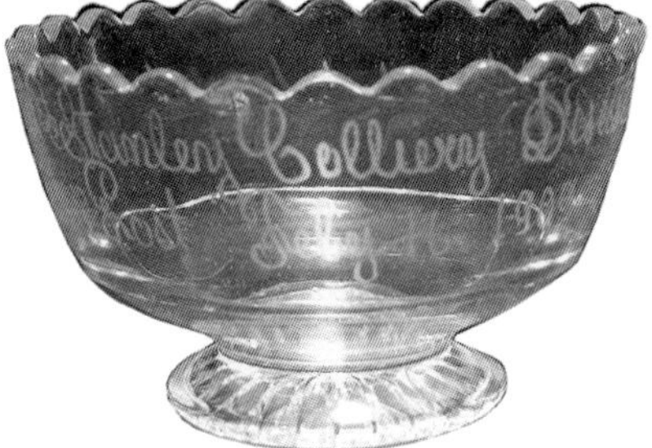

Table 1 Covers accidents and disasters in coalmines. It lists dates, the colliery involved, the inscription on the glass and at least one publication that reported the event. The letter in the final column relates to the key above and refers to the type or types of glass on which the incident is commemorated.

Table 2 Lists events relating to the mining industry where no loss of life was involved.

Table 3 Lists accidents not associated with mining but where loss of life was involved.

Table 4 Lists glasses that relate to individuals or events with a North Eastern association.

Table 5 The events of national importance in this list were generally recorded on glass manufactured in other parts of the British Isles but we believe that the glasses we have listed here were all engraved in the North East.

On page 93 we chart by date the glasses we have recorded 1840-1920. The 'gap' between 1865 and 1876 is evident, as is the huge increase in production 1891-1895.

TABLE 1   MINING ACCIDENTS

No	DATE	COLLIERY	INSCRIPTION	REPORTED	KEY
1	28.9.1844	Haswell	Haswell Colliery/ Explosion28 Sept 1844/ 95 Lost Their Lives	Durham Advertiser 11.10.1844	A
2	15.8.1848	Murton	Murton Colliery/ Explosion/ 15 aug 1848/ 15 lives lost	Temple, D. *Collieries of Durham v1*	A
3	19.8.1851	Washington	Washington/ Colliery Explosion/ 1851' 35 Lives Lost	The Durham Chronicle 22 & 29.8.51	A
4	2.3.1860	Burradon	Burradon/ Colliery Exp/ 2nd March 1860/ No 76	Thompson, R. A.E *How long did the ponies live?*	A, E
5	20.12.1860	Hetton	Hetton Colliery/ Explosion 20 Dec 1860/ 22 Lives Lost	Newcastle Daily Journal 22.12.60	G, D
6	16.1.1862	Hartley	Hartley Colliery/ Disaster Jany 16 1862/ 204 lives were lost	Illustrated London News 25.1.62. McCutcheon, JE *The Hartley Colliery Disaster*	A,B,D,E, F,G
7	8.9.1880	Seaham	Seaham Colliery/ Explosion/ 164 lives lost/ Sept 8 1880 (typical)	The Durham Chronicle 6.3 & 3.4.85	B,C,D,K
8	16.2.1882	Trimdon	Trimdon Grange/ Colliery Explosion/ Grange 16 Feb 1882/ 72 Lives Lost	The Durham Chronicle 24.2, 24.2, 31.3 & 7.4.82	E
9	02.03.1885	Usworth	In Memory of/ Usworth Colliery/ Explosion March 2nd/ 1885 (typical)	The Durham Chronicle 6.3 & 3.4.85	D,E,G,H K
10	02.12.1886	Elemore	Elemore Colliery/ Explosion/ 2 December 1886/ 27 lives lost (typical)	Temple, D. *Collieries of Durham v1*	A,D,E
11	10.11.1888	Seghill	Robert Barr/ who lost his life/ Seghill Colliery/ 1888	Blyth Weekly News 17.11.88	G
12	11.12.1889	Beamish	In Memory of/ Matthew Lee/ Who lost his life at the/ Mary Pit Beamish/ Dec 11th 1889/ Aged 23 year	www.dmm.org.uk	K
13	11.4.1891	Usworth	In Memory of/ William Bell/ Who lost his life/ By an Boiler Explosion/ At Usworth Colliery/ Aged 23 Years	The Durham Chronicle 11.4.91' 17.4.91, 13.5.91, 21.5.91	J
14	18.1.1894	Craghead	A Present To Kate Lumsdon/ In Memory of William Old/ Who lost his life At/ Craghead Colliery/ Jan 18th 1894 Aged/ 57 Years	The Durham Chronicle 19.1.94	D

No	DATE	COLLIERY	INSCRIPTION	REPORTED	KEY
15	13.7.1894	Barrington	An Alarming/ Accident Occurred/ at/ Barrington Colliery/ 13 July 1894	Newcastle Daily Journal 14.7.94	B
16	14.9.1894	Cambois	In Memory/ of William Beattie/ Who was killed at Cambois/ Colliery 14 Sept 1894/ Age 32 years	Blyth Bi-Weekly News and Wansbeck Telegraph 18.9.9	A
17	16.11.1894	North Seaton	In Memory of/ Edward Wilson/ who was killed at/ North Seaton/ 16 Nov 1894 age 23	Morpeth Herald and Reporter 17.11.09	A
18	8.4.1895	New Delaval	In Memory of John George Whitlock Who was accidentally Killed at New Dalaval (sic) Colliery 8 April 1895 Age 13 years 11 months. Gone but not forgotten	Morpeth Herald 13.4.95	B
19	25.4.1895	Dinnington	In Memory of/ Michael Lenneham/ Who was killed at/ Dinnington Colliery/ April 25th 1895/ Age 22 Years/ 1895	Newcastle Daily Journal 26.4.1895	A
20	12.7.1895	Broomhill	Gas Explosion at/ Broom Hill Colliery/ Hall was severely Burnt/ and O Brian escaped with his life/ 12 July 1895	Alnwick and County Gazette 20.7.95	A
21	13.04.1896	Brancepeth	In Memory of Brancepeth Colliery Explosion April 13th 1896	The Durham Chronicle 13.4.96	A
22	6.5.1897	Kelloe	Kelloe Colliery/ Disaster 6 May 1897/ 10 Lives Lost.	Durham Chronicle 7.5.97; Newcastle Daily Leader 7.5.97 et seq.	B
23	15.08.1899	Brandon	Brandon/ Colliery Explosion/ 15th Aug 1899/ 6 lives lost	Durham Chronicle 18.8.99	D,F
24	12.4.1903	Chester Moor	Boiler Explosion/ at Chester Moor/ Colliery/ April 12 1903	Durham Chronicle 17.4.03	A
25	16.11.1903	Sacriston	Robert/ Richardson/ Rescued alive/ after 91 hours/ Peril The Sacriston/ Disaster/ 3/ Miners Entombed/ Nov 16 1903	Durham Chronicle 27.11.03 et seq. Durham County Advertiser 11.12.03	I,D,E
26	15.7.1905	Bebside	Bebside Disaster/ 15 July 1905	Morpeth Herald and Reporter 22.7.05	F
27	14.10.1906	Wingate Grange	Wingate Grange/ Explosion/ 14 Oct 1906/ 24 Lives Lost (typical)	Durham Chronicle 19.10.06; Emery, N. *The Coal Miners of Durham*	A,G,D,H K

No	DATE	COLLIERY	INSCRIPTION	REPORTED	KEY
28	17.12.1906	Urpeth	Urpeth/ Colliery Explosion/ 17 Dec 1906	Durham Chronicle 21.12.06	A,G
29	19.3.1907	Benwell	In Memory of/ Richard Kirk/ who lost his life/ in Benwell Colliery/ Explosion/ March 19 1907/ age 55 years	Newcastle Daily Chronicle 20 & 22.3.07	D
30	7.5.1907	Whitburn	Whitburn Colliery/ Mystery Solved/ Overseers Body Found/ 1907	Shields Daily Gazette & Shipping Telegraph 8 & 9.5.07	A,D
31	20.2.1908	Washington	Washington Colliery/ Disaster/ feby 20 1908/ 14 Lives Lost	Durham Chronicle 28.2.08	D,G,J
32	9.1.1909	North Fallingsby	Explosion/ at North Fallingsby Colliery/ White Mare Pool/ Wardley/ William Moor/ Who Lost his Life/ Saturday January 9 1909	Newcastle Daily Journal 11.1.09	F
33	2.21909	Harton	A Serious Accident/ at Harton Colliery/ Several Men Badly Injured/ Feby 4 1909	Newcastle Daily Journal 5.2.09	D
34	16.2.1909	West Stanley	West Stanley/ Disaster/ 168 lives lost/ Feby 16 1909 (Typical)	Forster, E. *The Death Pit* 1969	E,D,G,H,J
35	16.2.1909	West Stanley	In Loving Memory/ of/ William Nicholson/ Who Lost his Life/ In the West Stanley/ Colliery Disaster/ Feb 16th 1909/ Aged 33 Years	Forster, E. *The Death' Pit* 1969	D
36	20.7.1909	Hartford	Cage Disaster/ Hartford Colliery/ 4 men killed/ July 20 1909. Reverse with W. Dickson 31, F. Robinson 37, A Clarke 44, John Sturdy 21	Morpeth Herald and Reporter 24.7.09	F,D
37	11.5.1910	Whitehaven	Whitehaven Pit/ Disaster/ 136 lives entombed/ 1910	Whitehaven News 19 & 26.5.10 Haig Colliery Mining Museum	E,G
38	21.12.1910	Hulton	Bolton/ Explosion/ 354 lives lost/ Dec 1910	www.bolton.org.uk/ pretoria pit.html	E
39	13.8.1916	Woodhorn	WOODHORN DISASTER/ AUG 13 1916 13 LIVES LOST	Newcastle Daily Journal 14.8.16 Morpeth Herald 18.8.16	C,D,J

TABLE 2   OTHER MINING RELATED INSCRIPTIONS

No	DATE	INSCRIPTION	SUBJECT MATTER	REPORTED	KEY
40	5.4.1844	The Strike/ of Durham Miners/ april 5th/ 1844	A strike against the 'bond' system that tied miners to a pit. It started in March and folded in August	Temple, D. *Durham Miners' Millennium Book*	B
41	1887	Northumberland/ Strike/ 1887	The collapse of the coal trade in 1886 and the end of the sliding scale of payment led to the strike settled in May with 12.5% cut in wages	Satre, L.J. *Thomas Burt, Miner's MP 1837-1922*	A
42	1892	Durham Miners/ Strike/ 1892	12 week strike against the advice of miners' leaders ended in June with 10% cut in wages	Emery, N. *The Coal Miners of Durham* 1992	A,B,G
43	1894	Better Luck/ To the Durham Miners/ 1894	See below		A
44	1894	Better Luck/ To the Northumberland Miners/ 1894	Probably in response to the severe depression in the coal trade and owners' demand for wage cut	Minutes Northumberland Miners' Mutual Confident Association 1893	A
45	13.1.1894	Northumberland Miners/ Advance of $7\frac{1}{2}$ Per Cent/ January 13 1894	An earlier offer of 5% rise in wages was increased to 7.5%	Morpeth Herald and Reporter 20.1.94	A
46	02.2.1894	Northumberland/ Miners First Pay/ of/ $2\frac{1}{2}$ per Cent/ Feb 2 1894	Probably related to the previous item		B
47	6.9.1894	The Memorial Stone/ Of a New Miner's Hall/ Was laid at/ Ashington Colliery/ 6 Sept 1894	A £3000 loan was offered by the Miners Mutual Benefit Society but withheld until concerns over the design were resolved. The money was paid on 16.3.95	The Miners' Mutual Benefit Society of Northumberland records	A
48	26.1.1895	Alarming Powder/ Explosion/ New Delaval/ 26 January 1895	Gunpowder, being kept in a miner's house, was accidentally ignited by hot coals. The house was damaged and two children injured.	Morpeth Herald & Reporter 2.2.95	A

No	DATE	INSCRIPTION	SUBJECT MATTER	REPORTED	KEY
49	10.10.1895	A Serious Fire Ashington Colliery on Saturday 19 Oct 1895 Accidents will happen	A fire in the miner's cottages belonging to Ashington Colliery destroyed 7 houses in 5th Row	Morpeth Herald and Reporter 26.10.95	A
50	1895	Success to Hartford/For 1895/ Drink Plenty Good Beer/ And Your'e Shure to Thrive			A
51	1898	NOW WEE SHANT BE LONG 1898	The circumstances not clear but almost certainly connected with mining		
52	30.7.1909	Coal Strike settled July 30 1909	Non-Union members who operated the coal trucks underground struck for higher wages. The Union got involved and the strike lasted several weeks.	Northumberland Miners' Mutual Confident Association minutes	E
53	06.4.1912	THE GREATEST COAL WAR/ THE WORLDS EVER/ KNOWN/ ENDED/ APRIL 6 1912	The largest coal strike in British history in support of a minimum wage. It ran from 1 March to end April after a bill to enforce a minimum wage was pushed through parliament.	Temple, D *Durham Miners' Millennium Book*	A, E, F
54	1914	GET BACK THE TWO SHIFT SYSTEM	A Bill passed in 1910 effectively changed the miners' two shift system to three shifts. In 1914 Northumberland miners failed to get a Bill through parliament to restore the earlier system.	Minutes Northumberland Miners' Mutual Confident Association	
55		Keep off/ The Black/ List	The Black List was used by employers in 19th and 20th centuries to deny work to miners thought to be agitators	Fynes, R. *The Miners of Northumberland and Durham*	E
56		Success to Burradon Colliery	The reason unclear but for history of the colliery see www.dmm.org.uk		

TABLE 3 NON-MINING ACCIDENTS

No	DATE	INSCRIPTION	SUBJECT MATTER	REPORTED	KEY
57	22.7.1880	In Memory of John Patterson Connell 22 July 1880	He was a joiner at Cambois Colliery. He got into difficulties while swimming was rescued but died later.	Morpeth Herald & Reporter 24.7.80	
58	16.6.1883	Victoria Hall/ Disaster June 16 1883/ 209 children lost there (sic) lives/ Sunderland	See page 24 for detailed report	Newspapers Ncle Daily Journal 18, 19 & 20.6.83	A,B,C
59	4.7.1894	In Memory of/ John Henry Todd/ Who was Drowned/ on the 4th July 1894/ at Blyth aged 23 years	A poor swimmer he went swimming at Cambois sands and got swept out by tide.	Morpeth Herald & Reporter 7.7.94	A,B,G
60	9.1.1895	In Memory of/ John & Thomas William Nobley/ Who were Drowned at/ Barrington Colliery/ Jan 9 1895/ Age 11 & 8 Years	Two sons of a miner fell through the ice on a reservoir belonging to the colliery. (Newspaper reported their name as Noble)	Ncle Daily Journal A 11.1.95	
61	13.7.1895	In memory of four Blyth Men/ George W Nicholson 22/ George Brown 30/ Thomas Brown 21/ George Dawson 30/ who were drowned/ 13 July 1895	The four men set out from Blyth in the *Marie*, a small sailing boat owned by George Brown. Weather was rough and they failed to return. The boat was found capsized by a passing steamer. None could swim.	Morpeth Herald A,B & Reporter 20.7.95 Blyth Bi-Weekly News 16.7.95	
62	26.9.1896	The Jarrow Boat/ Disaster 26 Sept 1896/ 7 lives lost	A small boat being used as a Jarrow to Howden ferry sank. The boatman and 6 passengers, including 2 women, drowned. One passenger, the only swimmer, and another who clung to the boat, survived.	Ncle Daily Journal G 28.9.96	
63	9.12.1904	New Biggin/ Disaster/ Dec 9th 1904	7 men from Newbiggin went to the rescue of Norwegian ship *Anglia*. Their coble capsized and only one was saved.	Morpeth Herald A,C,F,G & Reporter 17.12.04	

No	DATE	INSCRIPTION	SUBJECT MATTER	REPORTED	KEY
64	29.7.1905	Boating Disaster/ at CressWell/ 29th July 1905	Three miners on a fishing trip at night overturned their rowing boat. Two drowned.	Morpeth Herald & Reporter 5.8.05	C
65	24.8.1905	Disaster in Blyth Bay/ Fishing Boat Capsized/ 3 Men Drowned/ Aug 24th 1905	3 men and a dog were out salmon fishing when their boat overturned in a heavy swell only 200 yards offshore. The men were lost but the dog swam to shore.	Morpeth Herald & Reporter 26.8.05	D, E
66	4.2.1906	In Loving Memory/ of Lady Grey /Wife of Sir Edward Grey/ Who died as the result of/ a Trap accident /Near Alnwick/ February 4th 1906 'In the Midst of Life we are in Death'	Dorothy Widdrington became Lady Grey by marriage in 1885. She was driving her dog cart when the horse shied, the cart struck a tree stump, throwing her out and fracturing her skull. She was 41.	Morpeth Herald & Reporter 10.2.06	J, E

TABLE 4 OTHER LOCAL EVENTS AND DEATHS

No	DATE	INSCRIPTION	SUBJECT MATTER	REPORTED	KEY
67	3.8.1832	William Jobling Gibbetted at Jarrow Slake August 3rd 1832	A striking miner was involved in an attack on a magistrate who died as a result. He was sentenced to death and his body to public exhibition	Temple, D. *Durham Miners' Millennium Book*	A
68	5.11.1849	Prize fight on Blyth Links/ Between Stoke of Seghill/ and Mills of Gateshead/ Stopped by Police 1849	Two miners were engaged to fight but the authorities decided to prevent it after an earlier fight had resulted in the death of one of the men.	Newcastle Guardian 10.11.49	
69	7.7.1860	Robert Story/ The Northumberland Poet/ Died 1860	Born 1795 the youngest of 9 into a poor family at Wark Common he overcame adversity and rose to be a teacher/poet.	James, J. *The Lyrical … Poems of Robert Story with a Sketch of his Life.* 1861	A

No	DATE	INSCRIPTION	SUBJECT MATTER	REPORTED	KEY
70	18.8.1863	Time Gun Milburn Place/ Ballast Hill/ North Shields/ First Fired/ 1863	The first time it was fired by electric signal from Edinburgh Observatory on the occasion of the meeting of the British Association in Newcastle.	North & South Shields Gazette 27.8 & 3.9.63	
71	1879	Jesse Dawson Ewen/ St Mary's Island/ 1879	No evidence of this name apart rom a Jessie Ewen born in Newcastle in 1879.	1881 Census	C
72	7.1.1882	Violet Smith/ Died Jan 7th 1882 / at Seaham Colliery/ Aged 38 Years	The wife of a police sergeant. No details.	Durham Chronicle 13.6.82	K
73	1883	John Clavering/ Cramlington/ 1883	He is recorded in public records but no evidence of his death in that year can be found although a daughter was born in 1883.	1881 Census	C
74	21.8.1884	Albert/ Edward Dock opened 21 Aug/ 1884	Opened during an official visit by the Prince of Wales	Ncle Daily Journal 20-22.8.84	
75	5.11.1884	SS *Regian* Wrecked Upon The Bondicar Rock Between Broomhill and Amble 1884	A steam sailing ship on its way from Calcutta to Dundee ran aground in a storm but all the crew were saved.	Ncle Daily Journal 16.11.84	B
76	29.3.1885	John Graham/ Who Died March 29th 1885/ Through an Accident at/ Usworth Colliery/ Nov 28th 1884	The family claimed his death due to accident at the mine but death certificate records death due to rheumatism and pneumonia.	Death certificate	B
77	26.11.1885	In Loving Memory of/ My Dear Father/ Ralph Younger/ Died 26 Nov 1885/ Age 42 Years	Died of natural causes but death certificate notes he had a fractured spine of 8 years standing.	Death certificate	B
78	2.10.1889	In Memory of/ Thomas Wallace/ The Beloved Son of/ J and MA Willey/ Of White house Holmside / Who Died Oct 2nd 1889/ aged 25 years	A farmer's son 'accidentally shot by discharge of a gun carried by himself'.	Death certificate	A

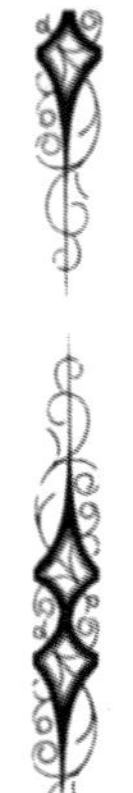

No	DATE	INSCRIPTION	SUBJECT MATTER	REPORTED	KEY
79	22.2.1890	In Memory of John R C Findlater / Died Feb 22nd 1890/ Aged 13$\frac{1}{2}$ Years	The son of a railway guard he lived in Philip St Newcastle and died of tuberculosis.	Broadfield House Glass Museum	I
80	2.4.1890	In Memory of Sarah Corliff, died 2 April 1890 (the name is incorrect)	The wife of a miner at North Seaton Colliery. She died, aged 67, of 'a severe cold age and exhaustion'.	Death certificate	K
81	4.8.1890	In Memory of/ David Wishart/ Who Died 4 Aug 1890/ Aged 29 years	Lived at West Pelton	Durham Chronicle 8.8.90	A
82	18.12.1890	In Memory of/ Mary Cook/ Who Died 18 Dec 1890/ Aged 75 Years	Wife of a miner at Pelton Fell died of bronchitis.	Death certificate	A,J
83	22.8.1891	In Memory of/ M Maddison/ Who died 22nd August/ 1891	A 21 year old who died of peritonitis & pregnancy complications.	Death certificate Morpeth Herald	G
84	25.11.1891	In Memory Of/ Robert Lancelot Booth/ Died 25 Nov 1891/ Ashington Colliery	Manager of the colliery for 14 years he died of a stroke aged 47.	24.11.91	A
85	29.12.1893	Edward/ Auberne Potter/ Died 29 Dec 1893/ Marine House/ Tynemouth	Colliery Manager and grandson of Edward Potter (1806-69) a mine owner at Cramlington.	Blyth Weekly News 6.1.94	B,G
86	1893	A Present to/ Laura Madden/ Born 9th July 1888/ From her/ Grandma/ 1893	Laura Madden born at Toppings Row, Boldon Colliery to James and Eliza Madden.	Birth certificate	E
87	1894	The Man Who Broke the Bank at Blyth 1894	John Robinson absconded after his bank, The Blyth Deposit and Advance Bank, failed he was never seen again.	Blyth Weekly News Morpeth Herald Ncle Daily Journal Feb, March & April	
88	1894	Better Luck to the/ New Biggin Folks/ Catch Plenty Fish 1894	Bad weather during the previous year seriously affected the fishing.	R.J. Martin *Newbiggin Lifeboat Station*	A
89	4.2.1894	In Memory of/ William Armstrong Scott/ who died 4th Feb 1894/ at Seaham Colliery/ Aged 73 years	Vicar of Seaham for 37 years and well regarded. He died of a stroke.	Durham County Advertiser 9.2.94	A

No	DATE	INSCRIPTION	SUBJECT MATTER	REPORTED	KEY
90	2.5.1894	Seaton Sluice/ Bridge Opened 2 May/ 1894	Replaced an existing toll bridge and was opened with much ceremony by Sir Matthew Ridley MP.	Morpeth Herald & Reporter 5.5.84	G
91	9.3.1894	Presented To/ Kate Lumsdon Upon her 19th Birthday/ from/ Mrs Old/ 1894	See Glass 14		D
92	29.5.1894	In Memory of/ Thomas Henry M Stratton/ Who Died 29 May 1894/ Cramlington House/ Age 42 Years	Highly esteemed colliery manager who died of pneumonia.	Morpeth Herald & Reporter 2.6.94	A,B, G
93	20.6.1894	Holywell/ Bridge/ Opened 20 June/ 1894	Carries the A192 across Seaton Burn, opened a few weeks earlier	No report found	A
94	11.8.1894	In Memory of/ Andrew Scott/ Of Broom Hill Colliery/ Who Died 11 Aug 1894/ Age 59 Years	He worked at Broomhill for 23 years rising to become manager. Work was suspended at the pit on day of funeral.	Morpeth Herald & Reporter 18.8.94	B
95	29.8.1894	William Holder Garrett/ Who Died 29 aug 1894/ Cowpen Quay Blyth/ Age 69 Years	Manager of the Central Co-op store he died suddenly of a heart attack.	Morpeth Herald & Reporter 1.9.94	A
96	9.12.1894	In Loving Memory/ of Eliza Willcock/ Who Died 9th Dec 1894/ Cambois/ Gone but not Forgotten	Died, aged 18, of acute peritonitis.	Death certificate	E
97	1895	In Honour Of Lord Walkworth (sic) Wishing him Success In the future 1895	Eldest son of the 7th Duke of Northumberland he entered Parliament in 1895, had a distinguished career in government and died in 1910 aged 39.		A,B
98	27.3.1895	In Memory of/ Anthony Toole/ Who Died 27 March 1895/ at New Hartley	He was a well regarded colliery mason who died, aged 33, of tuberculosis.	Morpeth Herald & Reporter 6.4.95	A
99	3.4.1895	In Memory of/ Nicholas Hoy/ Who Died 3 April 1895/ Age 35 Years/ Seaham Colliery	He was a checkweighman at the colliery and died of tuberculosis and exhaustion.	Durham Chronicle 12.4.95 death cert.	A,G
100	26.4.1895	Andrew Colvin/ Who Died at Blyth/ 26 April 1895 Age 84 Years	Started down the mines at the age of 9. At 32 he qualified as a Wesleyan preacher and became famous.	Blyth Weekly News & Wansbeck Telegraph 30.4.95	G

No	DATE	INSCRIPTION	SUBJECT MATTER	REPORTED	KEY
101	07.06.1895	Peter Young Waddle/ Who Died at Choppington/ Guide Post/ 7 June 1895/ Age 67 Years/	His name was actually Waddell and he died, aged 67, of a tumour, a recent amputation and congestion of the lungs	Death certificate	G
102	16.8.1895	In Memory of/ John Dickinson/ Died 16 Aug 1895/ Age 44 years	He was a miner who died suddenly age 41, of a cerebral haemorrhage.	Death certificate	A
103	22.9.1895	The Alnmouth Riot/22 Sept 1895 /Better Luck to the police/&/ The Rev Mr Brailford's (sic)/ recovery	An affray at Alnmouth. See page 44 for a detailed report.	Ncle Daily Journal 24 & 30 Sept. 7 & 8 Oct.. Morpeth Herald & Reporter 28 Sept. Alnwick Gazette 28 Sept	A
104	2.10.1895	In Memory of/ James Newton/ Died/ at Seaton Sluice/ 2 Oct 1895/ Aged 98 Years	He actually died on 1st Oct at 96. He was a gardener, domestic servant. Cause of death, senile decay.	Death certificate	E
105	1895	Success to Charles/ Fenwick MP/ 1895/ Re-Election Hee's a Jolly Good Fellow	Started life as a miner and in1885 was returned as MP for Wansbeck. Served for 32 years until health failed.	Ncle Daily Journal 22 & 24.4.1918	A
106	1895	Success to Thomas Burt MP Re-election 1895. Hee's a Jolly Good Fellow.	Elected as MP for Morpeth in 1874 and re-elected until 1918.		A
107	1895	Success To/ Prospect Terrace/ Amble/ 1895	The motive behind this is not clear. No Prospect Terrace in Amble now.		A
108	1895	Robertson (sic) Ewen/ St Marys Island	See page 36.	Shields Daily News 12.11.95	E
109	1895	Success to Stobbs Wood/ New Church/ The Good Shepherd/ 1895. (Reverse) auld lang syne	Probably the Chapel of the Good Shepherd at Stobswood Colliery.	N'land County Archive	A
110	4.6.1899	Isabella Vasey/ Died at Thames St./ June 4th 1899/ Age 101 years	The widow of a merchant seaman she died of senile degeneration. Thames St. no longer exists.	Death certificate	
111	13.8.1905	Time Gun North Shields/ Stopped Firing 13th Aug 1905D	See glass 70.		D
112	1934	T.B. Hindmarsh/ Blyth	Retired cashier, Cowpen Colliery, he died aged 82 of cardiac failure.	Morpeth Herald And Reporter 23.02.1934	C

TABLE 5 — NATIONAL EVENTS

No	DATE	INSCRIPTION	SUBJECT MATTER	REPORTED	KEY
113	1796	Death of Robert Burns 1796			B
114	1899?	The War England Always Ready	Probably start of Boer War.		
115	11.10.1899	Transvaal War/ Commenced 11 Oct/ 1899			B
116	1899	Transvaal War/ Three Cheers/ for General White/ at Ladysmith/ 1899	Refers to the siege.		B
117	1899	Transvaal War/ General Buller/ at the Front 1899			G
118	1900	Cheers for/ General Buller 1900			A
119	5.6.1900	Transvaal War British flag hoisted at Pretoria 5 June 1900			D
120	22.1.1901	Death / of Queen Victoria / January 22 1901			I
121	31.5.1902	Transvaal War Ended 31st May 1902			
122	20.6.1902	King Edward VII / Crowned 20 June / 1902.			E
123	6.5.1910	King Edward VII/ died May 6/ 1910			E, C, H
124	22.6.1911	Coronation/ of King George V/ June 22 1911			A
125	22.6.1911	Coronation/ of Queen Mary/ June 22 1911			A,E
126	1911	The New Reign/ of King George V/ June 1911.	Several variations.		E
127	15.4.1912	WHITE STAR LINE/ TITANIC SUNK	Variants		A,C
128	4.8.1914	THE WAR WITH/ England & Germany/ aug 4 1914			B
129	29.5.1914	Empress of Ireland Disaster May 29 1914	Collided with the Norwegian collier *Storstad* at the mouth of the St Lawrence river. Approx 800 died		
130	7.5.1915	THE LUSITANIA/ SUNK/ MAY 7 1915	Torpedoed off the southern coast of Ireland. 1198 died		B
131	5.6.1916	DEATH OF/ LORD KITCHENER / JUNE 5 1916	Died in the torpedoing of HMS *Hampshire* off Scapa Flow		C

A few unspecified records

No	DATE	INSCRIPTION	SUBJECT MATTER	REPORTED	KEY
132	1893	Merry/ Christmas/ 1893			A
133	1893	Its/ Very Canny/ 1893			A
134	1894	Tak/ A Wee Drappie 1894			A
135	1894	Home Sweet Home 1894			A
136	1896	Peace and Plenty 1896	This was a slogan that appears on late 19th century pressed glass wares commemorating W.E. Gladstone.		A,G
137	1900	Be Canny with the Sugar 1900			K
138		Health and Happiness			G
139		Never to Late to Mend			
140		Guid Auld Thornhill	Possibly of Scottish origin		G
141		Get your hair cut			A

TOTALS OF GLASSES IN A FIVE-YEARLY TIMESCALE

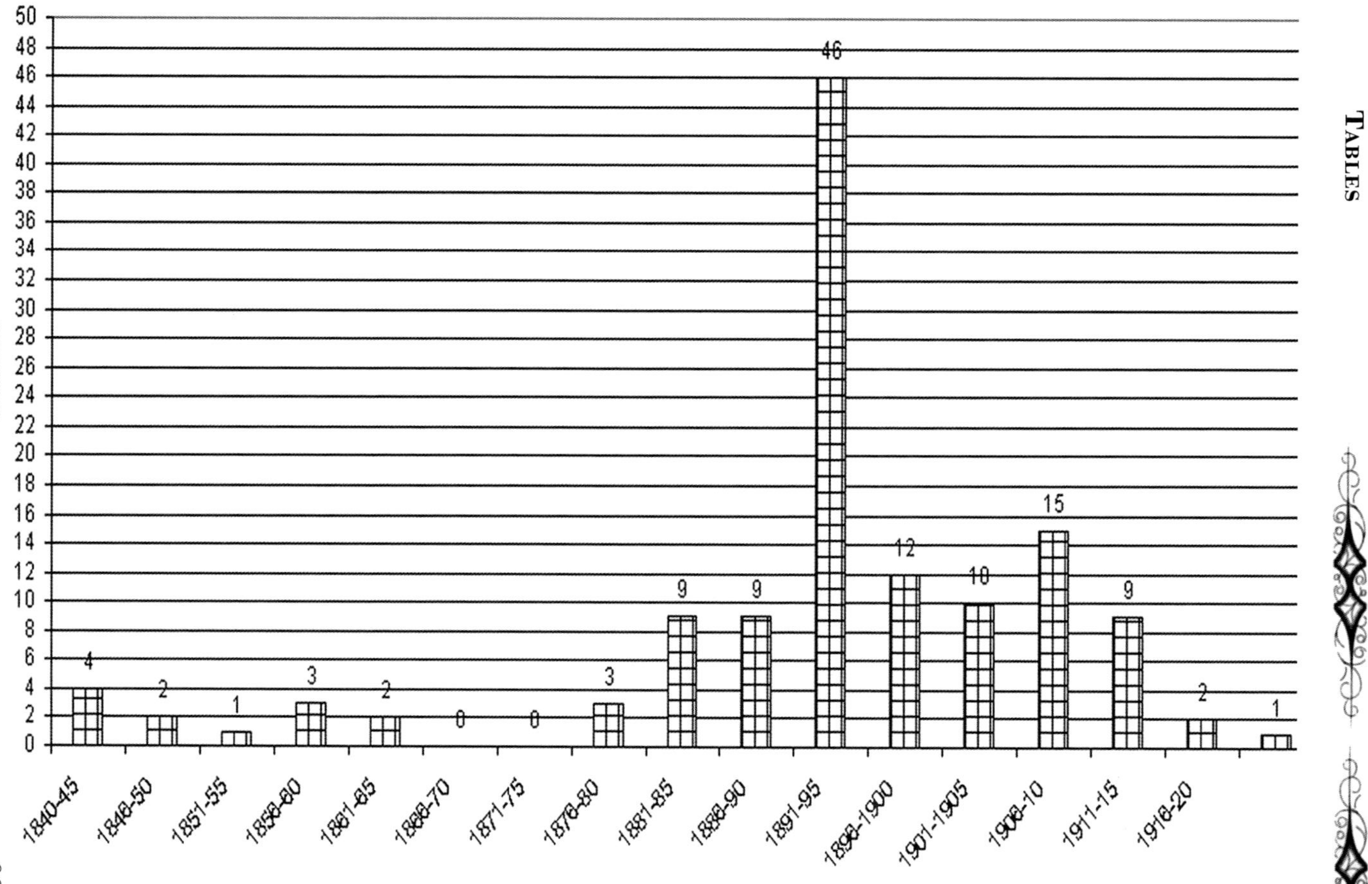

BIBLIOGRAPHY

Newspapers, periodicals and minutes

Alnmouth and County Gazette
Blyth Weekly News (published as Blyth Biweekly News and Wansbeck Telegraph, 1895-9)
Durham Chronicle
Durham County Advertiser
Illustrated London News
Minutes of the Hartley Colliery Disaster Relief Fund Committee
Minutes of the Northumberland Miners' Mutual Confident Association
Minutes of the Miners' Mutual Benefit Society for Northumberland
Minutes of Usworth Colliery Miners' Lodge
Morpeth Herald and Reporter
Newcastle Daily Chronicle
Newcastle Daily Journal
Newcastle Daily Leader
Newcastle Guardian
Shields Daily Gazette and Shipping Telegraph
Shields Daily News
Sunderland Echo
Sunderland Herald and Daily Post
The Times
Whitehaven News

Books and journals

Anon. *137 Steps: The Story of St. Mary's Lighthouse Whitley Bay*, North Tyneside Council, 1998

Atkinson, W.N and J.B. *Explosions in Coalmines*. Newcastle upon Tyne: Andrew Reid, 1886

Charleston, R. *English Glass and the Glass Used in England, c. 400-1940*. London: George Allen & Unwin, 1984

Collins P. *The Illustrated Dictionary of Northeast Shipwrecks*, Chester-le-Street, Collins and Brodie, Undated

Emery, N. *The Coal Miners of Durham*, Stroud: Allan Sutton Publishing, 1992

Fynes, R. *The Miners of Northumberland and Durham*, Newcastle upon Tyne: Davis Books, 1986, (Reprint; first published 1873)

Galloway R.L. *A History of Coal Mining in Great Britain* Newton Abbot: David and Charles Reprints, 1969 (Reprint; first published 1882)

Graham F. *The Death Pit*, Newcastle upon Tyne: Frank Graham, 1969 (Detailed account of the West Stanley disaster, 1909)

Greenwell G.C. *Glossary of Terms used in the Coal Trade*, Newcastle upon Tyne, Frank Graham, 1970 (Reprint; first published 1888)

Hajdamach C.R. *British Glass 1800 - 1914,* Woodbridge: Antique Collectors' Club 2003

Hunter R.W.G. *Saint Andrew of Blyth or Memorials of the Life of Andrew Colvin of that Town,* London: Rochdale Joyful News, 1897

James J. *The Lyrical and other Minor Poems of Robert Story with a Sketch of his Life and Writing,*

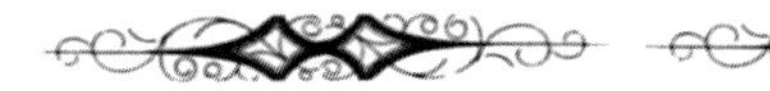

London: Longman, 1861

Kirkup M. *Blood on the Coal, A History of Woodhorn Colliery*, Woodhorn, WoodhornPress 1997

Lord W. *A Night to Remembe*r London: Longman's Green, 1956 (The classic account of the Titanic sinking)

Martin R.J. *Newbiggin by the Sea Lifeboat Station, The First 150 Years*, Newbiggin: R.J. Martin, 2001

Martin S.B. *Barrington Colliery Village,* Bedlington: Evan Martin, Bedlingtonshire Village History Series 1979

Massie R. *Dreadnought*, London: Johnathan Cape, 1992 (Detailed narrative of the events leading to World War I)

McCutcheon, J.E. *The Hartley Colliery Disaster 1862,* Seaham: E.McCutcheon, 1963

Pakenham T. *The Boer War*, London: Weidenfeld and Nicolson, 1979

Preston D. *Wilful Murder: The Sinking of the Lusitania*, London: Doubleday, 2002

Priestley J.B. *English Journey,* London: W. Heinemann, 1934

Robinson J. *Newbiggin-by-the-Sea: a fishing community*, Morpeth: Northumberland County Library, 1991

Rea V. *Jarrow Slake, A Photographic Record,* Jarrow: Bede Gallery 1988

Ross, C. *The North of England Bottlemakers' Strike of 1882-3* The Journal of the Glass Association, Vol. 1 1985

Satre, L.J. *Thomas Burt, Miners' MP, 1837-1922 The Great Conciliator,* London: Leicester University Press, 1999. (Chapter 7 is devoted to the 1887 strike)

Temple, D. *Above and below the Limestone. The pits and people of Easington District,* Newcastle upon Tyne: TUPS Books, Undated

Temple, D. *Durham Miners' Millennium Book,* Newcastle upon Tyne: TUPS Books, Undated

Temple, D. *The Collieries of Durham Volume 1,* Newcastle upon Tyne: TUPS Books 1994

Thompson, R.N. *How long did the ponies live? The Story of the Colliery at Killingworth and West Moor,* North Shields: Beacon House, 1997

Trevelyan G.M. *Grey of Falloden,* London: Longmans, 1937

Tuck, J.T. *The Collieries of Northumberland Book 1,* Newcastle upon Tyne: TUPS Books, 1993

Tuckman B. *The Guns of August,* London: Constable, 1962, (Chapter 1 is the classic account of the funeral of Edward VII)

Wamer P. *Kitchener. The Man Behind the Legend,* London: Hamish Hamilton, 1985

Wilson, J.H. *The Glass Industry of Tyne and Wear. Part 1 Glassmaking on Wearside,* Tyne & Wear County Council Museums, 1979

Wright I. *Alnmouth, Ancient and Modern,* Berwick on Tweed: Isabel Wright, 1995

Young R. *Shipwrecks of the Northeast Coast Vol 1 (1770-1917)* Stroud: Tempus Publishing, 2000

Internet

Dodds, E. Memories of Alnmouth: www.alnmouth.org.uk

Durham Mining Museum: www.dmm.org.uk (a very extensive database, not confined to the mines of Durham County)

Select index of names and places